Genesis

INTERPRETATION
BIBLE STUDIES

Genesis

CELIA BREWER SINCLAIR

WJK WESTMINSTER
JOHN KNOX PRESS
LOUISVILLE · KENTUCKY

First edition
Published by Westminster John Knox Press
Louisville, Kentucky

13 14 15 16 17 18 19 20 21 22—10 9 8 7 6

Scripture quotations from the New Revised Standard Version of the Bible are copyright © 1989 by the Division of Christian Education of the National Council of the Churches of Christ in the U.S.A. and are used by permission.

The photographs on pages 11, 30, 37, 43, 48, 51, 55, 57, 61, 64, 71, 74, and 82 are © 1998 PhotoDisc, Inc. All rights reserved. Used by permission. The illustrations on pages 6 and 40 are from Celia Brewer Sinclair, *Guide Through the Old Testament* (Louisville, Ky.: Westminster John Knox Press, 1989). Used by permission of the publisher.

Book design by Drew Stevens
Cover design by Pam Poll
Cover illustration by Robert Stratton

Library of Congress Cataloging-in-Publication Data
Sinclair, Celia B., 1954–
  Genesis / Celia Brewer Sinclair.
      pages cm. — (Interpretation Bible studies)
  Includes bibliographical references.
  ISBN 978-0-664-22967-2 (alk. paper)
  1. Bible. Genesis—Criticism, interpretation, etc. 2. Bible. Genesis—Textbooks. I. Title.
  BS1235.52.S56 2013
  222'.1106—dc23

                                                                    2013009916

Most Westminster John Knox Press books are available at special quantity
discounts when purchased in bulk by corporations, organizations, and special-interest
groups. For more information, please e-mail SpecialSales@wjkbooks.com.

Contents

Series Introduction

The Bible long has been revered for its witness to God's presence and redeeming activity in the world; its message of creation and judgment, love and forgiveness, grace and hope; its memorable characters and stories; its challenges to human life; and its power to shape faith. For generations people have found in the Bible inspiration and instruction, and, for nearly as long, commentators and scholars have assisted students of the Bible. This series, Interpretation Bible Studies (IBS), continues that great heritage of scholarship with a fresh approach to biblical study.

Designed for ease and flexibility of use for either personal or group study, IBS helps readers not only to learn about the history and theology of the Bible, understand the sometimes difficult language of biblical passages, and marvel at the biblical accounts of God's activity in human life, but also to accept the challenge of the Bible's call to discipleship. IBS offers sound guidance for deepening one's knowledge of the Bible and for faithful Christian living in today's world.

IBS was developed out of three primary convictions. First, the Bible is the church's scripture and stands in a unique place of authority in Christian understanding. Second, good scholarship helps readers understand the truths of the Bible and sharpens their perception of God speaking through the Bible. Third, deep knowledge of the Bible bears fruit in one's ethical and spiritual life.

Each IBS volume has ten brief units of key passages from a book of the Bible. By moving through these units, readers capture the sweep of the whole biblical book. Each unit includes study helps, such as maps, photos, definitions of key terms, questions for reflection, and suggestions for resources for further study. In the back of each volume is a Leader's Guide that offers helpful suggestions on how to use IBS.

The Interpretation Bible Studies series grows out of the well-known Interpretation commentaries (John Knox Press), a series that helps preachers and teachers in their preparation. Although each IBS volume bears a deep kinship to its companion Interpretation commentary, IBS can stand alone. The reader need not be familiar with the Interpretation commentary to benefit from IBS. However, those who want to discover even more about the Bible will benefit by consulting Interpretation commentaries too.

Through the kind of encounter with the Bible encouraged by the Interpretation Bible Studies, the church will continue to discover God speaking afresh in the scriptures.

Introduction to Genesis

The title of this first book of the Bible comes from the first word in the Bible, a word that means "beginning." There is endless scholarly debate as to which beginning is spoken of. Is it the origin of time, the origin of creation, or both? Regardless of the conclusion of that debate, Genesis is about beginnings—of the world, of a particular people, of a collection of holy writings known as the Torah, and of a sacred story common to several world religions. More importantly, however, Genesis is the story of a loving God who sets in motion both the beginning and the end.

"In the beginning"

Genesis contains many well-known stories, some of which have been told to us since our childhood. The images from these stories fill our mental museums—a Garden of Eden, an ark full of animals adrift in a flood, sneaky Jacob dressed up in animal fur to fool his father and steal his brother's blessing, and Joseph's dreams and his coat of distinction. These images have established the foundation for our own understandings of God. In a very real way, then, the book of Genesis is a beginning for our faith too.

Genesis is the *story* of one God and the *stories* of human experiences of that

> **Did Moses write the book of Genesis?**
>
> Perhaps Moses was a source for some of the material, but the book of Genesis as we have it today is more likely a combination of several sources. For more discussion of authorship and source theories, see William M. Ramsay, *The Westminster Guide to the Books of the Bible* (Louisville, Ky.: Westminster John Knox Press, 1994), 17–18; Bruce M. Metzger and Roland E. Murphy, eds., *New Oxford Annotated Bible: New Revised Standard Version* (New York: Oxford University Press, 1991), xxxv–xxxvi.

God. There are four main cycles of stories in Genesis: Creation, Abraham, Jacob, and Joseph. Within each cycle, the themes of God's creative power, God's presence and care, and the goodness of God's creation permeate the text. This study seeks to understand these stories and the story of the one true God, and what their message of faith is for us today.

Want to Know More?

About the book of Genesis? See Walter Brueggemann, *Genesis*, Interpretation (Atlanta: John Knox Press, 1982); John C. L. Gibson, *Genesis*, vols. 1 and 2, Daily Study Bible (Philadelphia: Westminster Press, 1981 and 1982).

About leading Bible study groups? See Roberta Hestenes, *Using the Bible in Groups* (Philadelphia: Westminster Press, 1983).

About source theory (JEPD)? See Richard N. Soulen, *Handbook of Biblical Criticism*, 2d ed. (Atlanta: John Knox Press, 1981), 58–59, 95–97, 113–14, 134–35.

Stories can have a variety of meanings, depending on how they are told and how they are heard. For the purposes of this study, some attempt has been made to allow the reader to feel what the characters in the story may have experienced. In this way, our individual faith stories become an extension of the biblical story. We are allowed the opportunity to discover ourselves as we participate in the pages of these stories. We understand the longing for the scents of Eden, we are humbled by the rainbow in the sky, and we affirm with Jacob that "surely God is in this place."

Several excellent commentaries exist on Genesis, foremost of which is Walter Brueggemann's *Genesis* in the Interpretation series from John Knox Press (1982). It is with appreciation to Brueggemann's work that this study is offered. The statement is fitting in this case that "the apple does not fall far from the tree."

The Creation

Consider these everyday uses of the word "myth":

"The movie has a mythic quality about it."
"The American dream is fast becoming the American myth."
"Mythical, sublime, majestic—the performance was truly memorable."

Fantasy, illusion, otherworldliness: such is the meaning of myth today. We think of myth as that which is beyond, or above, reality. My computer's thesaurus even lists "truth" and "fact" as antonyms of "myth" ("Do you buy that myth he told the boss?").

Now consider the associations we have with the word "science." Science (which includes scientific history) carries the weight of fact and certainty, of authority and white lab coats, of dates and precision. It's not a stretch to say that science today gives us the gospel truth.

As we enter the strange new world of the Bible, we are tempted to fall back on our old categories of experience to explain what we find there. We ask of Genesis 1:1–2:4a, a creation story, "Is it myth or science?" If the passage is mythical, then it speaks of that which is beyond (or above or beneath) material reality. If scientific, then the passage gives us concrete data and technique; it tells us how material reality came to be.

Covenantal Language

The text resists the either/or categories of myth or science. Myth looks at the god or gods apart from creation, whereas science looks at creation apart from the god or gods. But what we find in this passage is a strange, new way of perception. The speech of God should alert us to this fact: our simplistic, modern categories (be they literal, rational, or mythological) will not suffice. The text is in control here, not the enlightened reader, and it speaks good news that is understood on its own terms.

Fact or fiction?

As John Gibson points out, the real question is not whether or not Genesis is a *myth*, a term so loaded as to stir up more problems than it solves, but "How did people in an age thousands of years ago use imaginative stories like this?"—John C. L. Gibson, *Genesis*, Daily Study Bible (Philadelphia: Westminster Press, 1981), 12.

The language is "covenantal," insisting that meaning is not confined to God alone, nor to the world alone, but that the two are bound together. The text proclaims that Creator and creation are related in a decisive yet delicate way. The world has been given value by God, and the ultimate meaning of creation is found in the heart of the Creator.

The major themes we will explore are these:

"The ultimate meaning of creation is to be found in the heart and purpose of the creator."—Walter Brueggemann, *Genesis,* Interpretation, 12–13.

1. The text is to be read as liturgy. It is through speech that God calls those in exile (which includes us) to hear the blessings of God on all creation.
2. God establishes a special relationship with human creatures, who are God's stewards and made in the image of God.
3. God delights in this handiwork and proclaims it "good." The Sabbath is the satisfying culmination of this work.

The God of the Exiled

This creation story was addressed first to the exiled Jews in Babylon. The Jews understood their own "creation story" to have begun with Abraham (Gen. 11.30ff.), called out of anonymity in Ur of the Chaldees and promised the land and descendants that became Israel. God acted in history to create a chosen people. The story of the patriarchs and matriarchs told the Jews of their beginnings.

In the centuries before the exile, the Jews understood their god to be one of many and themselves as persons claimed by this god ("You shall have no other gods before me.") While Yahweh was indeed *their* god, other nations had their own deities. The infant knows the parent only as caretaker: one whose job it is to change diapers, feed, bathe, and comfort. The parent exists exclusively for the infant's care. So was Yahweh the God of Israel. Yahweh's relation to the rest of creation was simply not an issue.

But the great prophets of the eighth century (especially Amos) and the prophets of the exile (especially Second Isaiah) looked beyond the family circle. The patron deity of Abraham was the national God of Israel, to be sure. But this God was actually Lord of all nations, whether the Gentiles knew it or not. The parent has an identity greater than the child could ever imagine.

> "It is affirmed that the world has *distance* from God and a life of its own. At the same time, it is confessed that the world *belongs to* God and had no life without reference to God."—Walter Brueggemann, *Genesis*, Interpretation, 17.

The First Should Be Last

Our passage appears at the beginning of the Old Testament canon, but in a sense it should be read last. Its message reflects not a primitive, infantile understanding, but a fully developed and mature celebration of the character of God. It was late in the history of Israel, in the sixth-century crisis of exile, that the priestly editors and theologians set this creation story in writing. The liturgy that had circulated independently and orally for generations was finally codified so that the children of exile, who knew nothing of Jerusalem, would know their heritage. And the good news is this: the God of Israel is the Lord of all life, of creation itself. The parent has not abandoned the child in Babylon, because Babylon is God's domain and under God's dominion. What we read in this passage is a new perspective on who this God is, not just for a particular people, but for the entire world.

God is bound to creation; creation is bound to God. One cannot be understood apart from the other. The binding relationship is secured by the speech of God: "Let there be . . . It is good."

> "Using the same old materials of earth, air, fire, and water, every twenty-four hours God creates something new out of them. If you think you're seeing the same show all over again seven times a week, you're crazy. Every morning you wake up to something that in all eternity never was before and never will be again. And the you that wakes up was never the same before and will never be the same again either."—Frederick Buechner, *Wishful Thinking: A Theological ABC* (New York: Harper & Row, 1973), 18.

Genesis 1 tells of the decision of God to be alone no longer. God speaks to the waters of chaos and brings forth light and life. God speaks to the human experience of abandonment/exile and calls us forth into blessing and well-being. Such is the character of God.

Let There Be

The key metaphor for God's creative activity is speech (vv. 3, 5, 6, 8, 9, 10, 11, 14, 20, 22, 24, 26, 28, 29). Language flows from God, enlivening and animating the world. Language creates time itself ("Let there be light"), pushes back the primeval waters of chaos (the "dome" of v. 6, which the ancients conceived as a sort of plexiglass sphere keeping the water out), and brings forth dry land (a flat earth, of course, this being pre-1492). The point is not the technique and method, or whether we share the cosmology of the ancients, but the power of God's speech. God speaks something new that never was before. The means of creation is the very word of God.

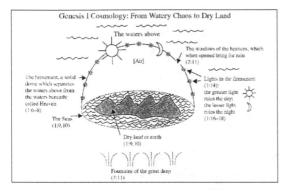

Celia Brewer Sinclair, *Guide Through the Old Testament* (Louisville: Westminster John Knox Press, 1989), 24.

Comparing our text with scientific (or, for that matter, creationist) theories is not helpful. It reduces the Genesis story to that which fits our sensibilities, be they modernist or literalist, and shows our disposition to control its meaning. But comparing the text to other ancient creation stories is illuminating. The great lights of the sun and moon, which Israel's neighbors in Egypt and Mesopotamia thought to be independent entities, here owe their existence to God alone (1:16). They are stripped of godly names; their status as deities no longer exists. Mesopotamian creation accounts give us a world emanating out of violence. A goddess is split in two, from stem to stern, her upper half forming the dome of the heavens and her lower half forming the earth. A god is bound by other gods and his arteries severed; the blood mixed with dirt forms the savage-creatures (humans). In contrast to this violence, Genesis 1 proclaims the stately, orderly, purposeful language of God, which serenely brings this good and bountiful earth into being.

The text is not interested in "how it happened." The "how" question pales alongside the questions with which the text is concerned: Who are we? Who is God in relation to the world? Genesis 1 is the proclamation of God's intent for us. The speech of God is hymnic, each stanza (or "day") beginning with "Let there be." The words are not commands. The author of creation is not authoritarian. "Let there be" leaves room for creaturely response (vv. 11, 24). The language is not coercive, but invitational.

"Let there be" denotes the graciousness of God toward all life and the entire world. There is both a closeness and a distance between Creator and creation. While speech binds God to the created order, this order is *not God* but separate and free. God causes all things to be, yet God lets them be. The author is not authoritarian any more than the parent is the tyrant. God cherishes creation, and in so doing God honors and respects it as well. God coaxes and invites, but as the host of this festive occasion God does not compel or coerce.

A "salvation theology" focuses on the reality of sin, of the creature's resistance to the goodness of God. Salvation theology is a powerful understanding of the distance and separation that exists between God and humans. But our text is evidence of an older and more venerable theology of blessing, or a "creation theology." Creation theology tells us that God has invested blessing into the operation of the world. God's blessings on the living creatures (1:22), on humankind (1:28), and on the seventh day (2:3) were given then and are given for all time. The gracious character of God means continual blessings on all of God's handiwork.

In the Image of God

The text moves with dignity and stateliness through the stanzas of the liturgy, the days of God's artistry. As the hymn swells, we note that God saves the best for last. At the end of the sixth day, "... in the image of God he created them; male and female he created them" (1:27). What does it mean to be created in the image of God?

We reflect God's image in many ways. In stark contrast to the static, perfect, Aristotelian notion of the Unmoved Mover, the biblical God shows emotion, movement, change. Both God and humans exhibit sadness, anger, gladness, joy. God loves, as do we. God speaks and acts, as do we. God creates, as do we. The Creator is reflected in the creativity of humans who give birth to children and ideas, homes and vocations, the arts and sciences, systems and communities.

The "image of God" is mirrored in our power over and care for creation. We are given responsibility over the created order to tend and secure its well-being. We have dominion over "the fish of the sea and over the birds of the air and over every living thing that moves upon the earth" (1:28) in the same way God has dominion over humankind. We have seen that God's speech is not coercive or demanding. God's dominion is characterized by caretaking. As Jesus put it, the one who rules is the one who serves (Mark 10:43–44). Humans, as co-creators, reflect the image of God. Our job is to see to it that we use our power responsibly. Our lordship over creation is manifest in good stewardship. Humankind, male and female, is given a commission to carry out the blessings of God in the world.

Want to Know More?

About covenant? See Donald K. McKim, *Westminster Dictionary of Theological Terms* (Louisville: Westminster John Knox Press, 1996), 64; Gordon S. Wakefield, ed., *The Westminster Dictionary of Christian Spirituality* (Philadelphia: Westminster Press, 1983), 98–99; Werner H. Schmidt, *Faith of the Old Testament: A History* (Philadelphia: Westminster Press, 1983), 106–9.

About the exile in Babylon? See Celia Brewer Sinclair, *A Guide through the Old Testament* (Louisville, Ky.: Westminster John Knox Press, 1989), 108–21.

About creation and science? See Shirley C. Guthrie, *Christian Doctrine*, revised ed. (Louisville, Ky.: Westminster John Knox Press, 1994), 145–65.

About human dominion over the Earth? See Jerome F. D. Creach, *Psalms*, Interpretation Bible Studies (Louisville, Ky.: Geneva Press, 1998), 68–76.

About Sabbath observance? See Rainer Albertz, *A History of Israelite Religion in the Old Testament Period*, vol. 2, Old Testament Library (Louisville, Ky.: Westminster John Knox Press, 1994), 408–11; Paul J. Achtemeier, ed., *Harper's Bible Dictionary* (San Francisco: Harper & Row, 1985), 888–89.

And It Was Good

The hymnic structure of the passage highlights God's *delight*. The refrain, "God saw that it was good," is repeated six times (vv. 4, 10, 12, 18, 21, 25). The hymn's crescendo is marked with the superlative "very good" as God delights in the creation of male and female (v. 31). The delight of God has its parallels in the great "Hurrah!" of Psalm 65 as the morning and evening, the hills and valleys, all together sing a great doxology. It recalls a time "when the morning stars sang together and all the heavenly beings shouted for joy" (Job 38:7). God is made happy by creation, and in response "the heavens are telling the glory of God" (Ps. 19:1).

With delight, God proclaims the goodness of creation. Again and again, "God saw that it was good." "Good" does not mean "perfect" or static and fixed, as when we say, "It's perfect;

don't change a thing!" Instead good carries the sense of that which is lovely, pleasing, beautiful. The "good" that God sees gives God satisfaction; it is consonant with the divine intention. The good is worthy of praise and doxology, so that even God is moved to appreciation of this fine work. The Sabbath denotes this, as it carves out a time in which first God, then the creation, may delight in what God has wrought. "That's good!" the parent says to the child, and the child beams back with joy.

A Day of Rest

The hymn of Genesis 1:1–2:4a ends with a great "amen": the institution of the Sabbath (2:2–3). The rabbis understood that on the Sabbath no one is to work or interfere with the created order in any way: no lifting, carrying, cutting, trimming, pruning. Creation can get along fine without us for one day, after all. Let it be!

We trivialize the Sabbath when we see it as a rest stop along the way of our busy lives, making it easier for us to work hard the rest of the week. As the late Jewish philosopher Abraham Heschel put it in *The Sabbath,* "The Sabbath is not for the sake of the weekdays; the weekdays are for the sake of the Sabbath. It is not an interlude but the climax of living" (14). The ending of this creation story proclaims that the Sabbath is part of the created order. It is not simply "down time," what's left over after all the items on the To Do list are crossed off. It is intentional and purposeful. On the Sabbath, we create what Heschel calls "a cathedral carved out in time."

It is the day of *menuha,* "rest," better translated serenity, peace, harmony. *Menuha* is the essence of the good life and a foretaste of life in the world to come (Heschel, 23). "The meaning of the Sabbath is to celebrate time rather than space. Six days a week we live under the tyranny of things of space; on the Sabbath we try to become attuned to *holiness in time.* It is a day on which we are called upon to share in what is eternal in time, to turn from the results of creation to the mystery of creation; from the world of creation to the creation of the world" (Heschel, 10).

> "The celebration of a day of rest was, then, the announcement of trust in this God who is confident enough to rest."—Walter Brueggemann, *Genesis,* Interpretation, 35.

We might imagine God on the seventh day, admiring and delighting in the world. The Sabbath is a deep sigh of contentment and ease, the joy of a job well done.

After the babies are christened at the Sunday service, the celebrants hold them up and parade them down the aisle. The congregation chuckles and grins, murmurs "Ah!" and "Look!" It is a Sabbath moment: one of pure joy. Well done! Such is the spirit of the creation story. Amen; so be it. Shout Hurrah! God said, "Let there be," and so it is. Hallelujah.

? Questions for Reflection

1. What does the word "myth" mean to you? Is it a good word or bad, a scary word or friendly? How can we use the word "myth" in connection with the biblical creation story, and still affirm our belief in that story?

2. This unit refers to the creative power of speech, particularly God's speech. The Greeks believed that the agent behind creation was known as the "Word." See John 1:1–6, which reflects a Greek understanding of creation. What connections can you find between the John 1 passage and this Genesis 1 passage?

3. How are we "in the image of God"? Whose image do people see when they look at you?

4. This unit quotes Heschel to say, "The Sabbath is a cathedral carved in time." What do you do on the Sabbath? How does Heschel's quote influence your understanding of the Sabbath?

Another Look at Creation;
The Temptation Story

If you draw a line dividing the text at the middle of verse 4 in Genesis 2, you see a dramatic change in setting, style, and story beginning with Genesis 2:4b.

The material in Genesis 1:1–2:4a is a doxology: a hymn of praise to the transcendent Creator and the good created order. The stanzas of the hymn are the seven "days." God's awesome power is expressed through language. "Let there be," so it is, "and God saw that it was good." The portrait of creation is carefully crafted. The language is stately and measured. God brings order out of chaos, pushing back the primeval waters to make light, sky, and dry ground. Vegetation, fish, fowl, and animals are called into being by God. God saves the best for last. The simultaneous creation of male and female "in the image of God" (1:27) is the crowning glory of creation. Humanity is given dominion or lordship over all that was created before, and the task of humankind is to be fruitful and multiply. The majestic hymn ends with creation of Sabbath time, when God and all the world stop to admire this good work. Sabbath is the great "Amen."

"In the day that the LORD God made the earth and the heavens . . ."

Dust to Dust

If the creation account of Genesis 1 is a doxology, what begins with Genesis 2:4b is a short story with economy of characters, action, and place. In contrast to the material in Genesis 1, we step into a barren world, parched dry (2:5). The primeval stuff is dust (Hebrew: '*adamah*) and the problem is not too much water, but too little. Springs rise up from below, clouds appear above, and an oasis is planted in the desert from which the rivers of life flow to the four corners of the earth. A male creature is formed first (Hebrew; '*adam*). He is patted into shape by God from the dust of the ground. God creates not by the magnificent word, but simply and by hand. The clay doll or earthling is animated by the breath (*ruach*) of God blown into the man's nostrils (2:7; in 1:2 the *ruach* is the spirit hovering over the primeval waters). To be alive is to have the breath, the spirit, of God.

Partners

Mirroring the command in Genesis 1 to have dominion, in 2:15 the human task is told in terms of stewardship. The man is to till and keep the garden (2:15), to tend the created order. But then the Lord senses that something is "not good": the male creature is lonely. The man is given animals as companions, to name and to care for. But wait; this companionship will not suffice (2:20) . . . God seems, with a scratch of the head, to ponder for a moment. The female creature is a better plan. Last but not least, she is formed (2:22). A partner is made, again by hand, created separately from the male creature. Together they exist in the little community of the garden.

"Woman is the crowning event in the narrative and the fulfillment of humanity."—Walter Brueggemann, *Genesis, Interpretation*, 51.

God is transcendent, omniscient, and deliberate in Genesis 1. In contrast, the picture of God in Genesis 2 is anthropomorphic, immanent, tentative; creation is a work in progress. If Genesis 1 is a fine oil portrait, then Genesis 2 is a photograph slowly emerging out of the chemicals in a darkroom. However, they stand by side in the biblical text, and we are to understand that both pictures are theologically true.

The anthropology, or view of humanity, is likewise complementary. Who are we? Genesis 1 answers that male and female, created simultaneously, together reflect the image of God. We are language creatures, like God. We are powerful and creative. With God we rejoice in the good earth and the creatures therein. Genesis 2 answers that we are made alive by the breath of God and formed with great care. This story describes the human vocation with a different emphasis, for while there is stewardship of the garden (and no command to be fruitful and multiply in Eden!) there is also prohibition. Not everything is permitted. There is a tree, and to taste its fruit is forbidden (2:17). As with any prohibition in any story, there is a hint of trouble ahead. The narrative is open-ended. What will the human creatures do with their freedom?

The narrative of chapter 2 continues without a pause into chapter 3, a drama set in the locale of the forbidden tree. God has delighted in creative activity, worked with the man to find a partner, and shown hands-on loving care. Tilling and keeping the garden is the human enterprise. Life is full. Aside from the etiology in 2:24, there is no interruption in the action or time to take a breath. But then the focus shifts from God's work to the initiatives of the human couple.

A Misunderstood Text

Genesis 3 is one of the most misunderstood texts in the Bible. In Christian traditions it has been used (following Augustine, and with the poetic imagery of Milton) to show the fall of humanity. Countless interpreters have employed this chapter as a proof text for the sin of pride and rebellion. Paradise is lost, we are told in Sunday school and from the pulpit, and someone is to blame. But what does the story say? First we should look at some assumptions and what needs to be cleared away.

The Bible is not controlled by Genesis 3. It is instead a marginal text. After Genesis 4:1, Eve is not mentioned in the Old Testament again. No allusion is made to Adam's sin except possibly Job 31:33. In Romans 5:12–21 and 1 Corinthians 15 Paul uses Adam as a type, by way of comparison and contrast, for Christ as the "new Adam." Nevertheless the role of the text is exceedingly limited. There is no reference to Genesis 3 in the prophets of the

> "All that they had been given was not enough. They wanted ultimate power, the power to be like God. . . . The only person who did not grasp at equality with God was Jesus (Phil. 2:5–8). . . . All other humans have failed."—Page H. Kelley, *Journey to the Land of Promise: Genesis-Deuteronomy* (Macon, Ga.: Smyth & Helwys, 1997), 18.

Old Testament or the Gospel writers of the New Testament. The fact is that the text is simply not central or decisive to the biblical testimony.

What we have instead are many misunderstandings of both the importance of the text and the way it is supposed to be interpreted. Let us begin by looking at some common misconceptions.

Genesis 3 makes no reference to a "fall." If we mean by "fallen" that, since Adam and Eve, humans are not capable of choosing the good, then we must ignore much that the Bible has to say. Cain is told by God that he may master sin in the very next chapter (4:7). Deuteronomy 30:11–14 assumes that humans are capable of obedience to God's purposes, and Joshua calls on the Israelites to "choose this day whom you will serve" (Josh. 24:15). In the great summary of true religion, Micah writes:

> "We've heard the fearful phrase 'fallen from grace.' But here is God's good news: We all, you and I, the whole human running race, have, by the mercy of God, fallen toward grace."—H. Stephen Shoemaker, *GodStories: New Narratives from Sacred Texts* (Valley Forge, Pa.: Judson Press, 1998), 26.

What does the LORD require of you but to do justice, and to love kindness, and to walk humbly with your God? (Micah 6:8)

These are not impossible demands. Humans are both required and able to do these very things.

This biblical anthropology is expressed in the Jewish teaching of the *yetzer ha-ra,* or inclination to do evil, and the *yetzer ha-tov,* or inclination to do good. Both are present in human nature. People are required to worship God with their *yetzer ha-ra* and their *yetzer ha-tov,* that is, with the whole self. Indeed the potentially aggressive and self-centered *yetzer ha-ra* can be marshaled and used for the good. The rabbis noted that without it, children would not be conceived, houses would not be built, business would not be conducted (Telushkin, 544). But we must work to develop the *yetzer ha-tov,* strengthening the inclination toward righteousness as we mature. Choices really exist. In other words, life outside the garden is problematic but not fallen.

The text does not explain the origin of evil. Nowhere in the Bible are we given theodicies or theories on this subject. Even in 1 Corinthians 15, Paul is not concerned with the origin of evil, sin, or death, but rather with the proclamation of the gospel. Such philosophical arguments and abstract statements are not the Bible's concern.

There is no devil in the garden to take the blame. The "Satan" in the book of Job is a member of the heavenly court, the prosecuting

14

attorney for God whose job is to patrol the earth. "Lucifer" is a name applied to a Babylonian tyrant by Isaiah in reference to his glory and pomp (14:12). These figures are absent from the narrative. If we wish to find Satan in the garden we must look to the Qur'an, where a rebellious angel is the trickster, rather than to Genesis 3.

> 📖 **Want to Know More?**
>
> **About the concept of the Fall?** See Shirley C. Guthrie, *Christian Doctrine*, revised ed. (Louisville, Ky.: Westminster John Knox Press, 1994), 221–27.
>
> **About cherubim?** See Walther Eichrodt, *Theology of the Old Testament*, vol. 2, Old Testament Library (Philadelphia: Westminster Press, 1967), 202–5.
>
> **About Satan?** See Shirley C. Guthrie, *Christian Doctrine*, rev. ed., 166–91 (and particularly 179–82); Walther Eichrodt, *Theology of the Old Testament*, vol. 2, Old Testament Library, 205–9.

Instead the Bible has a serpent, one of God's creatures. This creature functions as a technique to move the plot of the story. The serpent is simply described as "more crafty than any other wild animal that the LORD God had made" (3:1). The Hebrew for crafty is also translated "prudent," as in the book of Proverbs. The talking creature is shrewd, but hardly the embodiment of evil.

The text is not about sex, much less the identification of sexual intercourse with "original sin." Labor pains, both for the woman in childbearing (3:16) and the man in sweaty toil of the ground (3:17–19), characterize life outside the garden. But nowhere do we find sexual activity to be a curse. The fruits of intercourse (children) and of hard work (fields and vineyards) are indeed blessings, not curses. An honest day's work and bouncing babies are now part of the human drama. The idea that every child is born damned or that sex is evil is alien to the text.

Finally, many interpreters approach the text with a seriousness that it does not deserve. They look for the root of sin (a word that is not mentioned) and assign blame accordingly. The blame is then made part of a moral tale, as if the story were a timeless fable on the battle between the sexes. Let's look at some of the ways this has been done.

Who's to Blame?

1. Adam's problem was Eve. He listened to her voice (3:17, but what did she say?), became the first hen-pecked husband, and suffered for it. He was simply following orders (3:12). The moral of the story: He who listens to his wife is a fool. Beware of the woman who talks too much.

2. Adam's problem was Eve. If anything, his "sin" was that he loved her too much. He knew that her fate was death (2:17), and he could not bear to live without her. This Romeo-and-Juliet scenario has Adam ready to die with or for Eve out of his great but misplaced devotion. The moral of the story: Beware of too much love for another human being, especially a woman.

3. Adam's problem was Eve. He never knew what hit him; he was simply handed a fruit and he ate (3:6). He was clueless, tricked by a duplicitous Eve. The moral: Beware of the seductress. Women are wily and evil.

4. Eve's problem was her pride. She wished to be "like God" (3:5), which is not her lot in life. Hers was a true act of rebellion. She was aware of the consequences of disobedience, yet she arrogantly chose to reach beyond her human limits and grasp at the prerogatives of God. The moral of the story: Pride goes before a fall.

5. Eve's problem was her naïveté. She was not around when the prohibition was given to Adam (2:16–17), she has no knowledge of what it means to die, and she is no more culpable than a curious child entranced by the fruit's beauty (3:6). The serpent tricked her (3:13) by playing on her gullibility. The subterfuge is heinous, for she is an innocent while the serpent is crafty (3:1). Eve was set up and entrapped. The lesson here (if there is one): Life is not fair; no good deed goes unpunished.

6. The problem is theological talk. The serpent is the first creature to talk about God, and he engages Eve in this inappropriate discussion. He misrepresents God in 3:1 and Eve embellishes the command (adding "nor shall you touch it") in 3:3. "In the day that you eat of it you shall die," says God in 2:17; "You will not die," the serpent says in 3:4. The serpent speaks the truth here, for the day passes and the humans still live. He is technically correct but theologically dangerous. The moral: Beware of God-talk. Don't rationalize, just obey.

7. The problem is the desire for knowledge. Knowing good and evil (or all things) comes from eating of the tree (2:17; 3:5). Eve wanted to be wise, so she ate. Adam, fully aware of what is going on here, wants wisdom too. Adam calculates that Eve is the guinea pig who did not die, as promised in 2:17, so the coast is clear. Besides, she now has something he lacks; Adam desires for himself what Eve has. The moral: Ignorance is bliss. Too much knowledge is a dangerous thing.

The list goes on. Countering number 4, above, for instance, one might as easily say that Eve was not prideful enough. Had she asserted herself, she would have boldly and abruptly told the talking serpent to shut up and be gone. By politely deferring to the serpent's suggestions, she lacked the sense of pride and self-respect necessary to follow through on her convictions.

The range of interpretations is bewildering for some rather uncomplicated reasons. We long for a kinder, simpler world. Hope for Eden implies its existence. Paradise must be lost; perhaps it can be regained.

Another powerful reason for the dazzling array of interpretations is the nature of the text itself. Its characters are few and the narrative is terse. All we have here are a man, a woman, God, a mysterious tree, a talking snake. We have, for whatever reasons, both God's permission and God's prohibition. The scope is limited; we have noted that Genesis 3 is a marginal text. Yet it abuts those big heated issues over which humans have fought, evidently, from the beginning. What went wrong? Who is to blame? What should the woman have done differently? What

> "The Bible is not an answer book to all of the curious questions we may ask. Of very many such questions, we may, along with the Bible, be prepared to say, 'We do not know.' "—Walter Brueggemann, *Genesis, Interpretation*, 43.

about the man? Why did God include the tree in the first place? As Adam passed the buck to Eve (3:12) and Eve passed the buck to the serpent (3:13), most interpreters merely repeat this procedure.

Reading into the Text

But the text is not concerned with these questions and it admits no answers whatsoever. As far as interpretations go, the text allows for "all of the above" and yet "none of the above." Propositions and theories are reductionist; they are attempts to control the story to meet an agenda. Controlling the story is not our task. Our responsibility is simply to read and attend to what we hear. When we listen closely, we hear another kind of truth. And that truth is about our own perspective.

Psychology knows that what Peter says about Paul tells you more about Peter than it does about Paul. The history of biblical interpretation indicates that what Peter says about Genesis 3 tells you more about Peter than it does about Genesis 3.

To illustrate, patriarchal societies read of the need for hierarchy and the subordination of women (note how many of the interpretations above blame Eve for a "fall"). Feminists protest this agenda and read that in eating the fruit, Eve acted with great courage and wisdom. "Woman, the one who will house life within her, helps to generate this new, active, challenging life beyond Eden" (Niditch, 17).

Augustine read our text and Psalm 51:5, RSV: "in sin did my mother conceive me," and found a doctrine of hereditary original sin transmitted through the sexual act. (This was after he was forced by his mother, Monica, to leave his concubine and son.) Judaism and many Christian traditions do not see this at all. With its emphasis on the righteous God who commands obedience, Judaism finds no hint of oppressive original sin. Adam and Eve were indeed disobedient, but outside the garden possibilities exist for authentic action and righteousness that did not exist in the confines of Eden.

Listening to the Text

Whether the Fall is read as up, down, out, or simply falling short, rest assured that the interpreter tells us what his or her perspective already acknowledges to be true. How then is the reader to proceed?

The first and most difficult task of the reader is to separate and set aside what has been said *about* the text. The story is so familiar. Interpretations abound, whether illuminating or restrictive. It is time to read the text afresh.

Next, as we read (or better, hear) Genesis 3, we listen to what arises in the heart and the imagination. Thoughts and feelings pop up: fear, anxiety, consternation, our stereotypes about men or women or God. These we note with a nod of the head. What we recognize tells us something about ourselves; we will ponder this later. We will prayerfully reflect on how the text interprets us.

> "God's love for us supersedes our sinfulness."—Carol M. Bechtel, *Glimpses of Glory: Daily Reflections on the Bible* (Louisville, Ky.: Westminster John Knox Press, 1998), 9.

Then we read on to verse 21: "And the LORD God made garments of skins for the man and for his wife, and clothed them." And we notice that life goes on.

The story is finally about God and the way God responds to the human drama. The potter with the clay is also the seamstress with the garments: Button up your overcoat . . . you belong to me. Whether bumbling or arrogant, short-sighted or far-reaching, bold or fearful, we are God's. We are cared for and protected.

Our fig leaves (3:7) are pitiful; what we long for and receive is the finery of God's own making. To be clothed is to be given life (2 Cor. 5:4). The trial and sentence of Genesis 3:9–19 describes the reality of life. God struggles with the humans and decides finally to respond graciously, to clothe them with care. There is simplicity in the action and dignity in the effect. God does for them what they cannot do for themselves.

> "Our text leaves us with the hope that the creator is at work *renewing every day*."— Walter Brueggemann, *Genesis*, Interpretation, 44.

This little story has been overworked, made to play the part of a timeless moral tale or a tragic epic drama. But it concludes with the focus back on God's creative, simple action. The biblical story is just beginning, and the future is open-ended. God makes possible life, in its texture and richness, outside the garden.

Questions for Reflection

1. This unit affirms life as the handiwork of God. In fact, one of the quotes from this unit is: "To be alive is to have the breath, the spirit, of God." How does this statement speak to issues like capital punishment or hate crimes?
2. Adam and Eve struggle with choices, between the desire to do good and the desire to do evil. What guidelines do people use when they make a choice (difficult or otherwise)?
3. Seven ways this story has been interpreted are listed in this unit. Keeping those in mind, what would you say the story of the Garden of Eden is about?
4. This story, like much of scripture, may have become too familiar. It becomes hard to hear the story without also remembering everything else we have always associated with the story. What are ways that help you hear the biblical story as if for the first time?

3 Genesis 4:1–26

Cain and Abel

First off, let's go ahead and get it out of the way: *Don't murder. Practice self-control.*

Of course fratricide is horrible. Cain is a murderer, and in a sense all murder is fratricide. Cain's punishment is swift and just. Let that be a lesson to all. Having said the obvious, we can take up where many studies of this text leave off.

The focus of this text is not on a moral lesson, like some story out of Aesop's fables. To read the text with a moralizing eye is to flatten and simplify it. These points are made more clearly, after all, in the Ten Commandments and the book of Proverbs.

We have entered a "strange new world," and we do well to explore it fully. What interests the storyteller? Where are we drawn into the text? Our answer focuses us on the speech of God. This speech is found in two scenes: (1) In 4:6–7, God addresses Cain before the murder occurs. The subject is sin, and attention is paid to Cain's troubled state of mind. Cain is silent. (2) In 4:9–15, God addresses Cain in a trial after the murder of Abel. God questions, Cain answers, and a verdict is rendered. Cain responds in anguish to the sentence, and God responds to Cain, mitigating the punishment.

What do the speeches tells us? What are the real problems here? What is the relationship between the sibling issue (which is ethical and horizontal) and the mystery of God (which encloses theological and vertical issues)? We will look carefully at 4:1–16 for answers. Then, we will ask how this episode is linked to what comes before and after it.

A Sibling Rivalry

Humans have a competitive nature. Superpowers vie for economic supremacy. Ethnic groups try to establish whose ancestry is older, who has squatter's rights, what language is to be preferred. Lines in the sand are drawn between north and south in Korea, Vietnam, Ireland, the United States.

"How old are you?" children ask each other, and the six-year-old child knows she is somehow better than the one who is only "five and a half." Put any group of strangers together and they will exhibit subtle and not-so-sub-

> The story of Cain and Abel could be our story, speaking to temptations and feelings we all share. As Elizabeth Achtemeier says, "Like Cain, how envious we become of God's grace poured out on someone else." *Preaching from the Old Testament* (Louisville, Ky.: Westminster John Knox Press, 1989), 71.

tle ways of gaging who is the prettier, stronger, smarter, wealthier, more powerful. If there were only two people left in the world, they would compare belly buttons and the "innie" would declare himself superior to the "outie."

An Instigating God

Cain and Abel are brothers and, placed where they are in the narrative, the only two siblings around. Yet there is no hint of conflict between them. They are content to have different occupations (4:2). They come together in a simple act of worship (4:3–4). It is not until God steps in that a problem arises. Were it not for God, these two would be at peace. There is, standing above or between the

> "Life is unfair. God is free. There is ample ground here for the deathly urgings that move among us."—Walter Brueggemann, *Genesis*, Interpretation, 56.

brothers, that mysterious third party named "the LORD." And what an enigmatic presence! What puzzling behavior! God sets the competition in motion.

"And the LORD had regard for Abel and his offering, but for Cain and his offering he had no regard" (4:4–5). That is all there is to it. Commentators and readers turn back flips trying to make sense of this choice: God prefers sheep to fruit offerings, or shepherds to farmers, or God knew the hearts of both brothers and Abel's was purer. None of these explanations will suffice. No reason is given in this passage because there is none to give. God's regard for Abel and his offering is simply a fact of life. Such is the mysterious freedom of God.

Getting Even

"So Cain was very angry" (4:5). We can understand that. The choice was arbitrary. Life isn't fair. Whether Cain was angry at God, Abel, the system, or the situation is not stated; indeed he probably does not yet know the target of his anger.

Conventional wisdom says the human emotions are basically four: glad, sad, mad, and afraid. Look deeper, and we know that sadness is fear turned inward. Internalized fear becomes depression, listlessness, and ennui. Sad is the debilitating side of being afraid, while mad is fear turned outward. Angry persons are driven by fear to irritation and insult, bigotry and aggression. Anger is always a cover for fear, the most primal of emotional responses, and we do well to ask what it is Cain fears most.

A triangle exists between Cain, Abel, and God. In this particular instance God chose Abel. On another day perhaps God would choose Cain. But what if not? The future is uncertain here (as it always is). This is scary stuff. God initiated this particular choice for no particular reason whatsoever. Such is the freedom of God. Cain's face falls because he is alarmed. Created "with the help of the LORD" (4:1), Cain now fears the very Source of his life.

Challenging the Beast

God's first speech addresses Cain directly, perceptively, intimately. It is, in a sense, an answer to his fear. God immediately identifies Cain's anger for him (v. 6). Then (v. 7) God holds out two possibilities. Note that these choices are within Cain's control. First, "If you do well" means that the future is wide open. Cain may choose to do rightly, and God will accept him. Cain has this power, which God promises to bless. Second, after God graphically identifies for Cain the power of sin, God offers him a challenge and an invitation. The verb form of *timshel* is ambiguous: "you *must* master [sin]" is one translation;

"you *may* master [sin]" is another. God gives Cain counsel and information. More importantly, God expands the repertoire of responses available to Cain, opening up a future of real possibilities.

While Augustine saw "original sin" in Genesis 3, it is here in 4:7 that we have the first mention of the word "sin" in the biblical narrative. It is forcefully described: sin is like a wild beast, a hungry desert lion, hidden in cover of darkness by the door. You might think you are heading out for a breath of fresh air, when Wham! The beast pounces and the night will never be the same. Sin is not breaking the rules; the commandments have not yet been given. It is not missing the mark of perfection or righteousness or godliness; such a report card mentality does not do it justice. Sin is a force larger than life. It takes on a life of its own, and what it wills is death.

Who has not seen it happen? Everything is going just fine; a person steps out for a breath of air, and some inexplicable destructive force seems to take hold There's the politician who is at the peak of his career, the businessman who has no need to swindle the company, the star athlete who plays by the rules on the field, and Wham! We see them topple and self-destruct before our eyes. We shake our heads in amazement. What scandalous behavior! How stupid! How foolish! Just when he had everything going for him, he shot himself in the foot. Nightly, the six o'clock news bears witness to what the Greeks identified as a love of *thanatos*, the desire for death.

> "Here is a picture of virulent sin: it is a power that desires to have you. Sin is a hungry lion waiting, ready to pounce. In other words, Cain, your anger is a devourer and envy will eat you alive. You must master it or it will be your master."—H. Stephen Shoemaker, *GodStories: New Narratives from Sacred Texts* (Valley Forge, Pa.: Judson Press, 1998), 30.

In Genesis 4 we are led by the image of the wild animal who may tear us apart. Sin is a lethal power at work in our lives. What is amazing, then, is God's offer to Cain. "You may master it." Cain has power even over this murderous, aggressive force.

The choice he makes is tragic, whether it be a premeditated act or manslaughter (4:8). But it is still a choice. Other possibilities existed. In this first speech God challenges Cain, even taunts him. It's a gamble and the stakes are high. But the outcome is not predetermined. Cain is human, free, and able to win. He could arm himself with that knife by the door, or pick up a rock and hurl it into the night. He could turn on headlights and freeze the animal in its tracks. He could master the beast, wrestle with it deep in the dark side of his soul. But he is stony, sullen, and silent.

What he chose to do instead was to use a knife or stone against his only brother. Such is the logic of anger: find someone to blame! Throw a stone and you'll feel release! The real target of Cain's anger is this arbitrary God, but Abel is the convenient scapegoat. The murder is dealt with quickly. It is fear, clothed in anger, hurled at the brother.

A Brother's Keeper

The second speech of God is a trial wherein Cain is questioned and a verdict is given. "Where is your brother?" (4:9) echoes "Where are you?" of Genesis 3:9. While Adam admitted that he was afraid, Cain counters with the famous question, "Am I my brother's keeper?" God should know where God's favorite is. Cain's anger rages still.

His counterquestion is ignored. Instead God shouts, "What have you done!" (the exclamation point is closer to God's speech than the question mark). The blood (4:10) of the murdered brother cries out from the ground! The Hebrew word is in the plural—"bloods"—which the rabbis understood to mean the blood of Abel's unborn descendants as well. Cain is responsible not only for the victim, but for the generations coming from him whose lives he has also destroyed. Indeed, what has Cain done!

Cain is sentenced by God to wander the earth as a fugitive (4:12). The farming land, land near Eden and near God, has no more life in it for Cain. He quickly and rightly senses the horror of this verdict. In a cry of real anguish he exclaims, "My punishment is greater than I can bear!" He is divorced from all that truly matters: the good earth, the company of others, the presence of God. "I shall be hidden from your face." Abel was the scapegoat for Cain's anger toward God, but now Cain realizes he cannot live without this God. It is the hiddenness and mystery of God that first angered him because it scared him so. He identifies his true fear, which is to be bereft of God's presence. At last Cain speaks sincerely.

A Negotiating God

God is moved by Cain's plea. God responds and *the verdict is changed.* God responds to Abraham's haggling in Genesis 18:22–33 and to Moses' shaming in Exodus 32:11–14. In view of what humans have to say, God is open to taking a different way into the future. But the plea here isn't coming from Abraham or Moses, who were after all interceding with God on behalf of others. We aren't talking about the prayers of the righteous. We are talking about Cain, a murderer, who is concerned for his own skin. The mystery and wonder is that God really listens at all.

Yet God responds to Cain. God marks Cain as God's own forever. It is a permanent mark of God's guardianship and custody. While hardly a badge of honor, it is incorrect to read the "mark of Cain" as folklore has mistakenly interpreted it. It is neither a bull's-eye for hit men nor a brand of shame. The mark is a sign of God's continued protection and mercy, like the clothing in 3:21. God is in effect saying, "This mark tells the world you are mine. If anyone comes after you, he'll have to answer to Me."

What is the relationship between the sibling issue and the mystery of God?

> **What was the mark of Cain?**
>
> The use of this verse to support slavery or the submission of one race to another ignores the biblical witness. Even without a specific description, the text is clear that the mark signified God's protection, and not God's shame. Probably the mark was an easily recognizable tatoo, perhaps like that mentioned in Ezekiel 9:4. Some suggest that the mark may have identified Cain and his descendants as worshipers of Yahweh. For a complete discussion, see Claus Westermann, *Genesis 1–11*, Continental Commentary series (Minneapolis: Augsburg Publishing House, 1984), 312–14.

The metaphor of a three-sided figure, with God at the "top," is helpful. The triangle is the most stable of geometric forms (witness the pyramids) as long as the horizontal base is solid and the vertices meet at the apex. Cain's business is to connect horizontally, in relationship and reconciliation with the brother. It is also his business to connect vertically, to give his offerings to the Lord and to "do well" before God. When he chooses to do otherwise, the potentially stable triangle falls apart; the pyramid disintegrates into a rubble of murder and banishment.

Dealing with Envy

There is one other business Cain did not attend to, and that was the mastery of that lion "sin." He did not take the beast or himself seriously. He did not wrestle with the dark side within that wishes to have its way. An internal connection was called for ("you may master it"), but Cain did not listen.

There is always a triangle between siblings and the parent. "Mama always liked you best." "You were always Daddy's girl." If the spotlight turns on one (even for a second), the other cries "That's not fair!" or "Look at me too!" The biblical narrative speaks to this competitiveness with Jacob and Esau (Gen. 25:19–33:17) and, more poignantly, the prodigal and the elder brother (Luke 15:11–32). The elder brother hated the attention given to his wayward sibling, not because he hates parties or even because he hates the brother, but because *it was not attention given to him.* "You are always with me," the father reminds him. "All that is mine is yours" (Luke 15:31). Both of you are mine, and we have a homecoming here. I choose to throw a party; now come on in.

God says to Cain: Mind your own business, and mind it well. I choose to accept Abel's offering; that's my business. Your job is to do well before me and to be brother to Abel. This you can do; now let's get on with it. Never mind the spotlight on Abel. Both of you are *mine.*

In the New Testament, Matthew records a parable of Jesus which few can read without a twinge. It's the story of the laborers in the vineyard (Matt. 20:1–16). At the end of the day, the first-hour laborers grumble (read: the eldest child is vexed). They feel penalized; the landowner isn't being fair. How could he show such favoritism to these eleventh-hour workers? The landowner heaves a sigh and replies:

> Friend, I am doing you no wrong. . . . Am I not allowed to do what I choose with what belongs to me? Or are you envious because I am generous? (Matt 20:13, 15)

Indeed God's goodness can make us murderous, if we let it. But how God relates to the brother or sister, to other workers or worshipers, is not our concern.

📖 Want to Know More?

About the nature of sin? See Shirley C. Guthrie, *Christian Doctrine,* revised ed. (Louisville, Ky.: Westminster John Knox Press, 1994), 212–27; for a technical discussion of Old Testament perspectives on sin, see Horst Dietrich Preuss, *Old Testament Theology,* vol. 2, Old Testament Library (Louisville, Ky.: Westminster John Knox Press, 1996), 170–77.

About God changing a decision? See Terence E. Fretheim, *Exodus,* Interpretation (Louisville, Ky.: John Knox Press, 1991), 286–87; for a detailed discussion of the Old Testament presentation of humanlike attributes of God (including changing one's mind), see Horst Dietrich Preuss, *Old Testament Theology,* vol. 1, Old Testament Library, 244–49.

About God's name? See James D. Newsome, *Exodus,* Interpretation Bible Studies (Louisville, Ky.: Geneva Press, 1998), 15–25; Terence E. Fretheim, *Exodus,* Interpretation, 62–67; and James L. Mays, *Psalms,* Interpretation (Louisville, Ky.: John Knox Press, 1994), 65, 101.

About dealing with anger? See Carroll Saussy, *The Gift of Anger: A Call to Faithful Action* (Louisville, Ky.: Westminster John Knox Press, 1995), and Andrew D. Lester, *Coping with Your Anger: A Christian Guide* (Philadelphia: Westminster Press, 1983).

The Separation of Sin

How is this episode linked to what comes before and after it? Placed where it is in the morning of the world, the story of Cain and Abel intensifies the human problem first seen in the garden. If instead of "sin" we use the word "separation" (as Tillich does), the primeval stories of Genesis 1–11 show the spread of sin throughout the earth. Beginning in Eden, we see:

1. Separation between the humans and God ("I heard the sound of you in the garden . . . and I hid myself," 3:10)
2. Separation in the relationship between human lives (which is expressed in blaming and shame)
3. Separation between the humans and the earth ("cursed is the ground because of you," 3:17)

The separation between humans and God is deepened in Genesis 4. In response to God's first speech, Cain is silent. In response to God's question in the second speech, Cain is surly and insolent ("Am I my brother's keeper?").

The separation between human lives is deepened as well. While Adam and Eve's relationship is fractured, there is still life together outside the garden. With Cain and Abel we see that fractured relationships can become deadly. The ultimate separation between humans is murder. Within one generation, just one hour after the dawn of time, sin spread quickly, profoundly, and horribly. With Genesis 4 we know the reality of fratricide.

At the end of Genesis 3, Adam and Eve left the "automatic" earth of the garden. Henceforth Adam must work the soil with the sweat of his brow, and his connection to the earth is toil and

> "[Cain] picked his destiny for time to come. He is protected, but far from home and without prospect of homecoming."—Walter Brueggemann, *Genesis*, Interpretation, 61.

drudgery. In Genesis 4 the earth, like a living thing, can no longer bear the presence of the human being. The blood of Abel cries out from the soil like someone buried alive. The earth opened up its mouth to receive the blood and then closed it forever. Henceforth the ground will no longer yield to Cain (4:12). He will roam the land, leaving the area just outside of Eden and heading (geographically and metaphorically) even further away from the garden to the land of Nod, which means "Wandering."

27

Grace Abounds

> **When did the Jews learn God's name?**
>
> The mention in Genesis 4:26 (as well as 12:8; 13:4; 26:25) of invoking the name of the Lord stands in some tension with the story of the giving of the divine name to Moses. In speaking to Moses in Exodus 6:3, God confirms that though Abraham, Isaac, and Jacob knew God, they did not know God by the name Yahweh. The references in Genesis to invoking the Lord's name may be intended to show an early awareness and reverence for the God whose name was not yet revealed.

But the story is not over yet. In spite of the presence of sin in the world, the presence of grace continues. God marks Cain as God's own forever. Cain marries (4:17; see note at end of chapter). Cain and his wife have a son; indeed seven generations flow from Cain (4:18–22), paralleling the seven days of creation. The gift of life and family persists. The arts, here music and metal work, are born as well. Civilization is problematic but it is not cursed. Civilization and culture can be for us a source of vitality, after Cain's name (Hebrew: *qanah,* "to get, to create").

Finally, with the birth of Seth to Adam and Eve (4:25–26), the spirit of Abel is revived. The line continues through Seth to Noah (Genesis 5), making Seth the biblical link to the people of promise. Seth has a son named Enosh, and "At that time people began to invoke the name of the LORD" (Gen. 4:26).

Cain's anguished cry to God became, with Seth and his descendants, a call of praise and a summons to which God will respond. Life is problematic. We are beset with fears. Yet the human spirit continues to yearn for the God who continually meets us, wherever we may wander.

❓ Questions for Reflection

1. The actions of Cain we understand. Under the same circumstances, we probably would have the urge to act as Cain did. But God acts in unexpected ways with Cain. How does God respond to Cain in this story? What does this story affirm about God and God's dealings with humanity?

2. In part, this is a story about anger vented in violence. This unit states that "anger is always a cover for fear." Think of times when you get angry. What is the fear behind that anger? What are constructive ways to react to anger?

3. Both this unit and the previous unit (about Adam, Eve, and the garden) present stories in which the human participants make hard choices with dire consequences. What are some other similarities between the two stories, both on the part of the human participants and of God's reactions to them?
4. This unit includes the statement: "How God relates to the brother or sister, to other workers or worshipers, is not our concern." If that is so, what *is* our concern?

Note on Cain: The woman Cain marries and the enemies out there whom he fears present a problem for those who wish to read the Bible as recorded history. Clearly the editors of Genesis intended otherwise: scientific history was not their purpose. The richness and breadth of the text extend far beyond a mere chronicling of events. Those who insist on reading it as such find problems, but those problems are theirs and not the Bible's.

4 Genesis 9:1–17

God's Covenant with Noah

They were on their way to the funeral of their son. Back home, his first crayon drawings were still on the refrigerator door. He was a beautiful boy, happy and seemingly healthy. Then one morning, he didn't wake up. He went to sleep that night in his crib and the next day he was gone. The autopsy revealed a large brain tumor. The tumor could not be detected until it was too late.

As they drove to the cemetery two sad days later, the sky was gray and overcast. It seemed as if the whole world were in mourn-

ing. It's not supposed to happen like this, the parents burying their child rather than the other way around. As the rain began to fall, the grieving mother whispered, "These are the tears of God."

The flood story is read rightly when it is understood as the story of God's grief. Too often, and wrongly, it has been told as a tale of punishment. But the narrative of Genesis 6:5–9:17 should never be used as a model for divine judg-

ment. What is central in the story is the anguish in the heart of God, which moves God to a new reality in relationship to the entire earth.

Creation Corrupted

The narrative belongs to the primeval past of Genesis 1–11. It is a great sweeping story of God's loving work beginning with the creation of the world, and of the growing resistance of humans to God's good intent. Counting from Adam and Eve, we arrive at the tenth generation by the time of Noah. And what a time it is. The separation that began in the garden has deepened. The resistance of humans to divine graciousness has hardened. What was "very good" in Genesis 1:31 is now described in very different terms: "the wickedness of humankind was great in the earth" (6:5); "the earth was filled with violence" (6:11); "all flesh had corrupted its ways upon the earth" (6:12). We are so familiar with the story that this description seems inevitable. But for God the verdict was not inevitable at all. It wasn't supposed to be this way, this sorry state of evil.

> "This story is not concerned with historical data but with the strange things which happen in the heart of God that decisively affect God's creation."—Walter Brueggemann, *Genesis*, Interpretation, 74.

The command to "be fruitful and multiply" of 1:28 has resulted in the multiplication of sin and separation. The command to fill the earth and subdue it has led to an earth filled with enmity and violence. "And the LORD was sorry that he had made humankind on the earth, and it grieved him to his heart" (6:6). The flood that follows is the outpouring of the tears of God.

Rushing in with the combined weight of human sin and divine grief, the flood is the implosion of the created order. The dome called Sky (1:6–8), fashioned to keep out the watery chaos, collapses. The windows of the heavens open and the fountains of the deep burst forth and break their bonds (7:11). The limits provided in Genesis 1 to keep out the dark primeval waters no longer function. Instead, as with a deep groan in the heart of God, the deluge is vented and all the earth dissolves in salty tears.

The Gilgamesh Epic

There are other accounts of devastating floods in the ancient Near East. The Babylonian Epic of Gilgamesh is the best known, dating from the second millennium B.C.E. Polytheism being older than monotheism, this pagan epic predates the Genesis story. The similarities are striking. A survivor named Utnapishtim is chosen; he builds a boat and takes his family on board. The flood washes everything else

Key Terms

polytheism Belief in many gods

monotheism Belief in one god

away. Birds are sent out to mark the receding of the waters, and sacrifices are offered when the family disembarks.

Differences too are striking. This flood was the by-product of bickering among the gods and irritation over the noisiness of humans, who like teenagers are keeping the gods up too late. The god Ea chooses Utnapishtim simply to spite the gods' plan: no one was supposed to survive. Afterward the goddess Ishtar sets her lapis lazuli necklace in the sky, making it deep blue, so she won't forget the flood. And finally, both Utnapishtim and his wife are made immortal. He tells Gilgamesh his story to explain why he joined the assembly of the gods.

In contrast to Genesis 6–9, the Babylonian epic is told in the first person, and the grief is that of the survivor. On the seventh day as the storm subsides, Utnapishtim says:

> The sea grew quiet, the tempest was still, the flood ceased.
> I looked at the weather: stillness had set in,
> And all of mankind had returned to clay.
> The landscape was level as a flat roof.
> I opened a hatch, and light fell upon my face.
> Bowing low, I sat and wept,
> Tears running down my face.
>
> (Tablet 11, lines 131–37)

The Hebrew account is not merely a shift in perspective from polytheism to monotheism. It is a shift in focus from the pathos of the survivors to the pathos of God. Immorality and evil are of no concern to the gods in the epic, whereas the sorry state of humanity is what moves God to grief and to action. Noah is a remnant, a representative of new humanity. He is what God desires: a righteous person (6:9; 7:1).

A Troubled God

The narrative marks a decisive and irreversible movement in the heart of God. As it begins in 6:5–11, the content is a lawsuit against humanity and the tone is one of condemnation and anger. When it ends in 9:1–17, the content is a salvation oracle and the tone is one of assurance and forbearance. The intervening flood tells us that God has powerful ways of acting in the world. It highlights the seriousness of God, who has high expectations for humanity. God will not abandon these hopes, and so God saves a remnant. God remembers Noah, one who walks with God (6:9) as God intended from the beginning.

God is not the angry tyrant but the troubled parent. God is sorry, and God grieves. The Hebrew word for grief, *'asav,* first appears in 3:16, where it is applied to Eve. In new life outside the garden, the woman will now bring forth children in *'asav.* And as any parent knows, the pain of childbirth does not end when the delivery is over.

> "The evil *heart of humankind* (v. 5) troubles the *heart of God* (v. 6)."—Walter Brueggemann, *Genesis,* Interpretation, 77.

The parents watch as their daughter, the angel who used to dance around the house in her tutu and tiara, grows sullen and withdrawn. Adolescence baffles them; where does she get all this anger? They don't like the company she keeps, which just makes her more determined to meet up with her friends, telling her parents she's going to the mall. Once mall security called, saying, come get her; they were all caught shoplifting. Once they got an anonymous call telling them where to find her passed out, a botched attempt at suicide. Family therapy sessions generated nothing but temporary deafness on her part. Now her parents are waiting for a call from absolutely anyone, police included, just to know she's somewhere safe and unharmed.

Her last words to them, as she walked out the door and into a waiting car in the street, were chilling. "I can't stand living here anymore. I'm sick of your rules and I'm sick of you both. I hate my life." Stunned and angry, they had watched her go. "Don't come back until you've gotten some sense, young lady!" her father had shouted. She shot back: "Don't hold your breath." Now they wish they had grabbed her tight, shaken some sense into her, confined her to her room for the umpteenth time. They know she's heading for disaster and God knows where it will end. They could never have imagined, seventeen years ago in the delivery room, that their perfect infant would become this hostile, hardened young woman. Now she's gone, vanished into the night. And they are totally, completely undone.

The flood, which from the human side looks like judgment, is seen differently from God's side. The movement from God's side is always one of grief. It is forty days of outpouring before the grief subsides (7:17).

A Change of Heart

In Genesis 9:1–17, which parallels 8:15–22 in structure and theme, the crisis is past. The little entourage, a microcosm of the new order, is ready to emerge. God commands: "Go out of the ark. . . . Bring out with you every living thing" (8:15, 17). All flesh is to abound, once again, on the earth. God has not given up; God is now ready to try again.

Genesis 9:1–7 is a regal speech. It begins with a blessing, followed by commands for the future after the flood. The speech of God shows that Genesis 1 is still operative. "Be fruitful and multiply" (1:28) is restated in 9:1 and 9:7. The image of God in 1:26–27 is claimed again in 9:6. Humanity is given fresh rule over the creatures, although now those animals and birds and creeping things must bear this rule in "fear and dread" (9:2). In 1:29 only green plants were given to humans for food; in 9:3 every moving thing that lives is given; the peaceful vegetarian diet is no more. But because blood (9:4) is equal to life, the post-flood world is reminded that God is the source of all life, and killing animals can never be taken lightly. Responsibility is heightened. Murderers will be directly accountable to God: "I will require a reckoning for human life" (9:5). The saying of verse 6 expresses an exalted view of human life, because human life images that of God.

Genesis 9:1–7 must be heard along with 8:21. The image of God persists in humanity, but what also persists is humanity's stubborn resistance to God's design. Incredibly, the flood story that begins: "every inclination of the thoughts of their hearts was only evil continually" (6:5), concludes the same way: "the inclination of the human heart is evil from youth" (8:21). As it was in the beginning, so it is in the end. God is fully aware that on the human side, nothing has changed.

> "There may be death and destruction. Evil has not been eradicated from creation. But we are now assured that these are not rooted in the anger or rejection of God."—Walter Brueggemann, *Genesis*, Interpretation, 84.

Yet God declares that what has happened will never recur. God will never again destroy every living creature. Genesis 9:8–17 moves from God's commands ("you shall") to God's promises ("As for me . . . "). As the laws of 9:5–6 are binding on all humanity, so the covenant of 9:9–11 is established with the whole world. Fulfilling the promise of 6:18, the Noachic covenant moves from Noah and his family, reaching out to the ends of the earth and to all generations after the flood. It is an unconditional promise and it stands forever: "Never again."

The Judean exiles and we who feel estranged from God today are reminded by Second Isaiah:

> Just as I swore that the waters of Noah
> would never again go over the earth,
> so I have sworn that I will not be angry with you. . . .
> [M]y steadfast love shall not depart from you,
> and my covenant of peace shall not be removed,
> says the LORD, who has compassion on you.
>
> Isa. 54:9, 10

Evil, death, destruction all exist in creation, but these are not rooted in God's anger or rejection. Instead, God pledges to bear the human lot alongside us, suffering along with us, assuring us that disaster and exile are not the last word.

The wind (*ruach*) blows over the face of the earth and the windows of the heavens close tight again (8:1, 2), but nothing has changed. There is nothing new under the sun, which is baking the mudflats dry. Yet something momentous has occurred. What has happened with the flood is a change in the heart of God. The deep grief of God has enabled God to move past anger and God's inclination to punish. God will stay with this world. The curse of the ground in 3:17 and the enmity between the bloody ground and Cain in 4:11 are gathered up and set aside: "I will never again curse the ground because of humankind" (8:21). God's persistent love overrides the sorry state of the earth. Humans tend toward evil and self-interest rather than goodness and altruism; in this sense they are hopeless. God will no longer be disheartened and surprised by this. God is moved to patience and forbearance, which God was not aware of having before.

Hosea 11:1–9 shows this same shift in the consciousness of God. It is a soliloquy that moves God to a new awareness. The passage begins with the moving memory of the child Israel: "I took them up in my arms. . . . I led them with cords of human kindness, with bands of love. . . . I bent down to them and fed them" (11:3, 4). God had literally hugged Israel out of Egypt. God continued to call Israel's name with love. But Israel grew up and turned away. The more God called, the less they listened. They became sullenly deaf to God's cry. They wanted more than anything to leave. God should give them up and let them

---

Want to Know More?

About Gilgamesh? See John Van Seters, *Prologue to History: The Yahwist as Historian in Genesis* (Louisville, Ky.: Westminster John Knox Press, 1992), 58; Walter Beyerlin, *Near Eastern Religious Texts Relating to the Old Testament*, Old Testament Library (Philadelphia: Westminster Press, 1978), 91–97.

About other ancient stories of the flood? See Paul J. Achtemeier, ed., *Harper's Bible Dictionary* (San Francisco: Harper & Row, 1985), 312–14.

---

go their willful way of destruction. By any measure, in any human court of law, Israel is guilty. But God will not judge by human standards. Out of grief a new resolve is born in the heart of God:

> My heart recoils within me;
> my compassion grows warm and tender.
> I will not execute my fierce anger . . .
> for I am God and no mortal,
> the Holy One in your midst,
> and I will not come in wrath.
>
> Hos. 11:8, 9

God Remembers

The law of *karma,* fate, is embraced by both Western and Eastern cultures. In the East, it is the one absolute law of the universe, unbreakable and unbendable: All actions have consequences, if not in this life then in the next. In the West, folk wisdom teaches that "You reap what you sow," and "What goes around, comes around." Indeed when that boomerang called fate hits us squarely between the eyes, we often recognize that it came flying out of our own hand.

But *karma* does not govern what happens in Hosea 11 and in Genesis 6–9. The law of cause and effect would dictate that God give up Israel for Hosea. It would mean that there would be neither Israel nor anyone at all after the flood. Yet Hosea 11 and Genesis 6–9 powerfully tell of a short circuit in the flow of divine judgment. These passages move from judgment to pathos with a break in between, a crisis in God's heart. What causes the break is the remembering of God. There was once sin and violence, and there still is sin and violence. But God remembered Noah (8:1), and now there is a re-creation and a covenant with the whole earth.

Remembering (Hebrew: *zakar*) is an act of committed compassion. God is not preoccupied with God, but with creation. The remembering of God makes new life possible. The flood, like the holocaust, is a time of amnesia. But the flood waters will not have their way. We cannot be ultimately forgotten, for with God we are eternally known.

Before the flood, God remembered Noah (8:1). After the flood, God will remember the everlasting covenant (9:16). The sign of the rainbow is both a promise to all creation and a reminder to God of the vow, "Never again." The newness is not in the created order. The new thing is in the heart of God. God has decided to put up with the world, and not just to put up with it but to stand with it. The bow, a weapon of war, is at rest. God's creation is forever protected from God's impatience. God is committed to finding another way to deal with unruly, hostile humanity.

The Noachic covenant is upheld by God unilaterally and unconditionally. This covenant operates independently of the community of faith; all people experience the peace of the rested bow whether or not they have heard of Genesis 9. This covenant makes the future possible. And it provides the context for more particular promises that will follow.

In the tenth generation after Noah came Abraham, God's particular choice in the post-flood world. Abraham is able to engage God in a remarkable debate on behalf of Sodom and Gomorrah (18:22–33), whereas Noah is apparently unable to speak up on behalf of a world that is about to be flooded. Noah does what God commands (6:22; 7:5) and shows that obedience is still possible. But Abraham's righteousness is of a different sort. God makes a special covenant with Abraham, and God declares that he is made righteous through faith (15:6).

God decides not to come in judgment, but to come to us in love. After the flood, beginning with a particular people, it is faith and compassion that binds God to humanity. In time, God is finally able to conceive a future when "No longer shall they teach one another, or say to each other, 'Know the LORD,' for they shall all know me, from the least of them to the greatest, says the LORD; for I will forgive their iniquity, and remember their sin no more" (Jer. 31:34). God will wipe the slate clean but not with the flood. The tears of the deluge become the tears of compassion as God suffers with us, gathering up the baby, the unruly teenager, the grieving parents, into the everlasting arms.

? Questions for Reflection

1. Many cultures retell a story about an ancient flood that covered the earth. In your opinion, is the flood story one of punishment, grief, or something else? Why?

2. What are the conditions of God's covenant with Noah? What are the requirements of Noah and what are the promises of God?

3. Along with the rainbow, the image of a dove with an olive branch in its mouth is one of the most enduring from this story. What does a dove or an olive branch usually symbolize? In what contexts do we normally see those symbols? How does this story influence those contexts, and how do those contexts color this story?

4. In this case, it was the heart of humanity God hoped to change, yet it was the heart of God which changed. What possibilities does this story suggest for someone facing a conflict or disagreement?

The Covenant with Abram

"**S**hall we dance?"

The question calls up images from *The King and I,* with Anna and the king of Siam (who will always be Yul Brynner) sweeping across the floor, Anna's full skirts billowing. We might think of a perfectly synchronized tango, a *pas de deux,* or a peppy, jumpy jitterbug. "Want to dance?" is the greatest icebreaker of all. It marks the end of the girls-on-one-side, boys on-the-other scene in the school gym. It means the beginning of movement, be it a waltz or swing or disco. The question alone gets our attention.

In a poetic way, "covenant" is dance. Covenant may be understood as a dynamic, ever-changing movement between two partners, initiated by God. God asks, humans respond, and the dance together begins.

The Call of Abram

Genesis 15:1–21 tells the story of the covenant between the Lord and Abram (see also the parallel in Genesis 17). Let us set the scene. Who are the players? Where is the action? What does God say to set the covenant in motion?

Abram appears on the stage without much fanfare and very little introduction in Genesis 11:27. Genesis 1–11, the primeval history that precedes his entrance, tells the story of origins: the beginnings of the world, of the good created order, of humanity, and of sin. The stage is huge, for God is dealing with the whole earth. Genesis 6:5–9:17 tells of God flooding the earth to make way for a new humanity with Noah, and finding that the same old song is playing: both before and after the flood, "the inclination of the human heart is evil from youth" (8:21; parallel in 6:5). In the aftermath of Babel, both humanity and sin are strewn across this vast stage. And then Abram enters.

He is called out of Ur in Sumer, out of the relative ease of early civilized city life with its understanding that many gods command the universe, each with its own domain. Ur belonged to the moon god

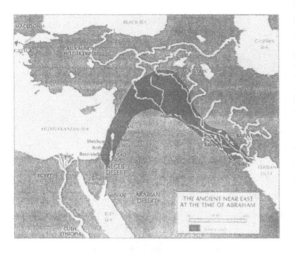

(incidentally, called Sin). The Sumerians could boast of running water and the beginnings of a written alphabet. Abram and his people could have enjoyed a pleasant and rather uneventful life there in the Fertile Crescent. But instead this Yahweh spoke to him, showed him the dance card, and said: "Go from your country and your kindred and your father's house to the land that I will show you" (Gen. 12:1). While Noah was chosen because he was "a righteous man" (6:9), the mystery is that Abram was chosen at all. The reason is simply "because" (compare Deut. 7:7–8).

The mystery is also that Abram responded. He moved off the sidelines and stepped out on the dance floor. Without knowing who this God was, he loaded up family and provisions and started on a magnificent journey. The story of Abram is the creation story of the chosen people.

The Promise to Abram

It is as if God has decided to deal, not with the whole earth and all at once, but with an individual people and a bit at a time. The spotlight is on Abram. God will work to solve the problem of sin, not with a huge Broadway revue, but a tiny intimate *pas de deux.*

The threefold promise issued to Abram involved these things:

1. Land: "Go . . . to the land that I will show you" (12:1); "all the land that you see I will give to you and to your offspring forever" (13:15)

2. Descendants: "I will make of you a great nation" (12:2); "I will make your offspring like the dust of the earth; so that if one can count the dust of the earth, your offspring also can be counted" (13:16)
3. The whole earth: "in you all the families of the earth shall be blessed" (12:3)

The wanderer will have a home: a land later called Israel, the promised land. This land will be filled with his offspring, a mighty nation. Finally, by or through these people, all other nations of the world will receive the blessings of God. Abram is like a funnel through whom Yahweh pours blessing that will cover, as was intended in the beginning, the whole earth.

> "Why and how does one continue to trust solely in the promise when the evidence against the promise is all around? It is the scandal that is faced here. It is Abraham's embrace of this scandal that makes him the father of faith."—Walter Brueggemann, *Genesis*, Interpretation, 140.

It becomes clear early in the Abram narrative that the second part of the promise, the part about the descendants, is problematic. Abram and Sarai are childless (11:30), and they aren't getting any younger. He follows local custom, cited in Hammurabi's Code of the same period, and takes a slave named Eliezer as his legally adopted heir. There appears to be no other way. Such is the situation when God meets with Abram in Genesis 15.

The Discussion between God and Abram

The structure of the text is worth noting. There are two sections: verses 1–6 are concerned with the faith of Abram, verses 7–21 narrate the binding in covenant. Looking closely at the first section, we see this movement:

> God's promise (v. 1)
> Abram's protest (vv. 2–3)
> God's response (vv. 4–5)
> Abram's acceptance (v. 6)

This section, especially the conclusion in verse 6, is the most important in the Abram narrative. Paul used it to reform Jewish understanding of faith, and all great reformers since have found the passage crucial as well (Augustine, Luther, Barth). It begins with an introduction and a promise; it ends with acceptance. Shall we dance? God asks, and after some discussion, Abram accepts the offer.

"The word of the Lord came to Abram in a vision." We think of words as auditory experience, visions as that which we see. But here the speech of God is the content of the vision. The conversation is rapid-fire, staccato, until the momentous pause (take a breath!) concluding with "he believed the LORD."

> "Only the new awareness that God really is God provides ground for Abraham's safe future."—Walter Brueggemann, *Genesis*, Interpretation, 143.

Between the threefold promise of 12:1–3 and the interchange of 15:1–6 there has been a gap in time, and during this gap Abram has no doubt pondered the futility of the promise. Nothing has happened, and he is afraid. "Fear not!" God begins. "I am your shield"—your protector, the one who keeps you safe. There's a reward in all this, and it depends on Abram's acceptance.

Continuing the metaphor of the dance, the "reward" is the dance itself. We can either stand here, each in our own little world, frightened and afraid of what the future holds, or we can create a future together. The reward is not merely a prize, although it can include that, a trophy gripped with sweaty hands after the winners have been announced. This sort of recognition will be his, surely. That has already been promised (12:1–3): land, posterity, blessing to the world. The reward is also the dance, the covenant, the experience itself. Will Abram trust his partner? Will he accept the offer?

Abram's Request

Abram asks for a sign: "O Lord GOD, what will you give me?" (v. 2). How is he to know the future is safe, the promises real? Their experience together has been short; they do not know each other well. This God has made a magnificent proposal involving a plan for the future. But the barrenness of the present has persisted. There is no heir. Waiting, biologically speaking, just makes matters worse. If you want to have offspring, you do not put it off until you are older and wiser. The couple is merely older and less likely to conceive. There are three major causes of infertility, the wise doctor says: age, age, and age. What hint can God give that this wisdom is mistaken?

"Count the stars." This is the sign, which is a clue to God's movement seen in everyday reality. "So shall your descendants be." Not the descendants of Eliezer, the adopted heir. Not the descendants (later) of Ishmael, Abraham's son through Hagar the Egyptian maid. Both adoptions were legal, both common practices. Neither was God's intent. Abram is to abandon his practicality and common sense, and to trust. He is to let himself be led in the dance that is covenant, no matter how exorbitant or extreme the moves might feel to him at the time. And the idea of counting the stars is the hint. It is absurd to try to do so, absurd to think the descendants will one day be as many as these twinkling lights, and that's the sign. "So shall your descendants be." And Abram believed.

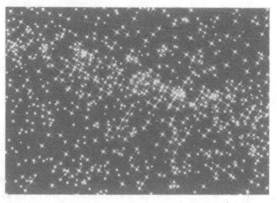

"Count the stars."

The Righteousness of Abram

For Abram, and for many of us, the present is dull, monotonous, deathly. The faith of Abram means moving out of the present, off the sidelines or the comfortable chair, and into the future. To trust God's future is a revolutionary action because everything changes. The Greek word is *metanoia*, or radical change. This belief of Abram tells us what it means to be human, what we are created to be. Abram is now a believer, or one who literally *does* belief. He holds on tight and waits for the cue; he rests in the arms of the promise giver.

Further, this "belief" tells us what it means to be righteous. Abram is now reckoned—not credited, as on a tally sheet, but designated—"righteous." This is not a falsification of the account books, a wink and "we'll just overlook this debt, maybe move it in the credit column." Righteousness involves doing justice to a relationship. Abram did just that when he believed, when he fell back into the arms of God in trust.

> "Faith is better understood as a verb than as a noun, as a process than as a possession."—Frederick Buechner, *Wishful Thinking: A Theological ABC* (New York: Harper & Row, 1973), 25.

This faith is what God had always had in mind. Faithfulness is what God intended from the beginning. It is trust that stands in sharp contrast to shame and guilt (as in the garden), to anger and fear (as with Cain), to ceaseless activity (as with the tower of Babel). Entering into the covenant is entering into the dance. This movement is now called "righteousness."

Abraham in the New Testament

It is in this sense that the New Testament letter of James follows our text:

> You see that faith was active along with his works, and faith was brought to completion by the works. Thus the scripture was fulfilled that says, "Abraham believed God, and it was reckoned to him as righteousness," and he was called the friend of God." (James 2.22–23)

The letter of James understands that works make faith possible, or (following our metaphor) that it takes two to tango. Entering into the covenant is not simply nodding the head, thinking or feeling a certain way, or saying OK to the offer. "Works" are the bodily, incarnated way of acting on the promise. Works are the dynamic movement of the dance.

Verse 6 is also central to Paul, as seen in Romans 4 and Galatians 3. For Paul, faith and works stand in contrast: it is by faith alone that we are justified or made right before God. God's gracious action preceded anything that Abram did, and the word of promise creates Abram's faith. Faith is recognized as the new righteousness.

Sola Fide

"Faith alone": Paul's affirmation of Abraham's example was the rallying cry of the Protestant Reformation.

Nevertheless Paul's argument fits our metaphor of the dance, because Paul's point is that God's blessing belongs not to those who perfectly obey the law but to those who live in faith, accepting God's free gift of grace. It is not for us to execute the moves perfectly, for God knows we must learn as we go. We will trip and step on some toes. Faith is the attempt to trust in spite of our clumsiness. And as Paul knows all too well, God's word can be resisted. We can decline the offer and sit out the dance instead. God's gracious invitation is not coercive. It is freely and mysteriously given; it is freely and often falteringly received. The faith that makes righteousness is acceptance.

Cutting the Covenant

The second section of our narrative follows this outline:

God's promise concerning land (v. 7)
Abram's question (v. 8)
Covenant ceremony (vv. 9–17)
    an ancient ritual act (vv. 9–12, 17)
    historical reflection (vv. 13–16)
God's promise concerning land (vv. 18–21)

This entire section is a dramatic affirmation of the covenant. The substance of the promise is land; indeed what good are the countless descendants if they have no place to live? Where is the dance to occur if there is no stage, no ballroom? Thus Abram's question: How is he to know that he will possess the land?

His answer is a ceremony, an ancient ritual. The ceremony is shrouded in mystery. It is initiated by God, who tells Abram to do some rather concrete things. Abram brings the animals and prepares them; he makes ready for the action to begin. Then all goes dark: the sun sets, deep sleep falls on him, terrifying darkness envelopes him. This is a sacred moment. Whatever happens in verse 17 is told with great restraint: smoke and fire penetrate the darkness and pass between the animal pieces. The Lord is not seen, but God's presence is clear.

Perhaps Jeremiah 34:18–20 sheds some light on what occurs here. In this rite, participants passed between divided animals and solemnly sealed, or "cut," the agreement (covenant). The fate of the slaughtered animal will be the fate of anyone who transgresses the covenant. The promise is enacted in liturgy, which involves both words and physical acts.

Verses 13–16 give the content of the promise. "Know this for certain." The only sure things are death and taxes; here God says the other certain thing is waiting. These verses anticipate the book of Exodus, a story of bondage and waiting. It will seem long; indeed when one waits it is always for too long. But a return to the land of promise is assured: "they shall come back here." Abram is the first to know this plan, and he may rest assured

> "The problem of faith is waiting. . . . But gifts may not be forced. Futures stay in the hand of the God who gives them."—Walter Brueggemann, *Genesis*, Interpretation, 149.

of it. A good old age is his to savor and he will die in peace.

The promised future is a long way off. Abram will wait for an heir during his lifetime, and it will be generations more before the land is theirs to possess. How tempting it is to construct a future of one's own, over which one has some modicum of control, if for no other reason than to keep us busy in the meantime. Take the lead in the dance; the partner is too cumbersome. Better yet, cut loose and go solo.

Waiting, following the partner's lead, seems restrictive or it makes us feel silly. Why bother? A pause in the action, in combination with a promise that seems too big to believe, is cause for taking matters into our own hands. In our Western world, "He who hesitates is lost," and "If anyone is going to get the job done, it must start with me." When the topic is waiting, these are surely the only words of wisdom our culture has to offer.

And so the speech of verses 13–16 is essential to Abram's faith and crucial to those who wait. It contains enough detail about the interim period to sustain the waiting process. God's speech, opened up by Abram's question, deals with a specific situation. We are creatures of time and place: God addresses Abram directly with timing (vv. 13–16) and place names (vv. 18–21). "What will you give me?" and "How am I to know?" are questions God takes seriously.

In the interim, the narrative continues. The faith of Abram and the faithfulness of God are the narrative's issues, thematic partners in a biblical ballet. Can Abram trust? Is his God a God who can be trusted?

The folding chair on the gym floor is hardly comfortable, but it will do. The band is actually pretty good, which is nice, because it looks like it's going to be a long night sitting here. Maybe it's time to stretch the legs, take another trip across the crowded gym floor to the bathroom. Just then, out of nowhere, comes a wink and the most wonderful smile:

"Shall we dance?"

📖 Want to Know More?

About righteousness? See Alan Richardson and John Bowden, *The Westminster Dictionary of Christian Theology* (Philadelphia: Westminster Press, 1983), 507–8.

About Hammurabi? See John Bright, *A History of Israel*, 3rd ed. (Philadelphia: Westminster Press, 1981), 58–59; Paul J. Achtemeier, ed., *Harper's Bible Dictionary* (San Francisco: Harper & Row, 1985), 370–71.

About the tension between faith and works? See Paul J. Achtemeier, *Romans*, Interpretation (Atlanta: John Knox Press, 1985), 76–85; Pheme Perkins, *First and Second Peter, James, and Jude*, Interpretation (Louisville, Ky.: John Knox Press, 1995), 112–14; Shirley C. Guthrie, *Christian Doctrine*, revised ed. (Louisville, Ky.: Westminster John Knox Press, 1994), 314–28.

About covenant? See Donald K. McKim, *Westminster Dictionary of Theological Terms* (Louisville, Ky.: Westminster John Knox Press, 1996), 64; Gordon S. Wakefield, *The Westminster Dictionary of Christian Spirituality* (Philadelphia: Westminster Press, 1983), 98–99; Werner H. Schmidt, *The Faith of the Old Testament: A History* (Philadelphia: Westminster Press, 1983), 106–9.

? **Questions for Reflection**

1. In this unit the metaphor of a dance describes the covenant between God and humans. What are some other metaphors that can describe the relationship between God and humans?
2. This encounter between Abram and God is similar to that of Moses and God (Ex. 3:1–4:17). What are some of the similarities in the two encounters?
3. Abram and God perform a ritual in verses 9–17 to seal the covenant, to close the deal. What are some of the things people do today to show the seriousness of their commitment, or to seal a promise?
4. Abram makes some risky decisions. What would inspire you to make similar risky decisions?

6 Genesis 18:1–33

God Visits Abraham and Sarah; Abraham's Intercession

Peekaboo! I see you!

It's one of the first games we play with babies. As soon as a baby's eyes are able to focus, it's a sure thing that some adult will sit with knees together to support the child's head and shoulders. He will point his toes on the floor to tilt the baby up and cover his face with both hands (hold that pose a second!), then pull the hands apart and say something nonsensical. The baby giggles and chortles in the most infectious manner. Perhaps it's nature's way of teaching serious grown-ups to be utterly silly.

It's the unexpected that makes us laugh. The pair of hands opens up to reveal a big grinning face. The magician pulls a rabbit out of a hat. The dignified gent with a bowler hat and cane is really a clown slipping on a

banana peel. Laughter can be the note that signals recognition. The world is not what we suppose it to be. We have been given new information that moves and disturbs us, but finally gives us delight.

Genesis 18 tells of God's visit with Abraham and Sarah (vv. 1–15) and of a conversation between Abraham and the Lord concerning the fate of Sodom (vv. 16–33). The stories are best read aloud and with a twinkle in the eye. The tone of each is playful and creative. In Genesis 18, we enter the realm of the unexpected.

Placed side by side, the two episodes form a diptych. They share common elements: theophanies and strangers, hospitality and bold questions. Both narratives brush aside that which is serious, conventional, and pragmatic. The diptych of Genesis 18 opens up new possibilities for Abraham and Sarah (vv. 1–15) and new possibilities for God (vv. 16–33).

> A **diptych** is something comprised of two matching parts, for example, two pictures that are hinged together.

Revisiting the Promise

As chapter 18 opens, Abraham is taking his siesta in front of a tent. The tent is pitched by the oaks of Mamre, just north of Hebron in the land of Canaan. Inside the tent is Sarah. Her Hebrew name means "Princess"; God gave her this new name at the sprightly age of ninety (17:15). We will step inside the tent and examine what is going on from her perspective.

It has been a long journey over time and space with her husband Abraham. They migrated with Terah, Abraham's father, and Lot, his nephew, out of the Fertile Crescent years ago, settling for a bit in Haran, where her father-in-law died (11:27–32). From then on it was just the three of them. Sarah was unable to have children. Being called "barren," empty, bothered her at first. But what could she do? Her life seemed full enough; besides, they were on the move again. A mysterious "LORD" had called them to go to Canaan (12:1–3).

That was twenty-four years ago, she thinks, knowing that numbers literally don't count for much. In the meantime they took a detour into Egypt, where she was as shocked by Abraham's behavior as she was pleasantly surprised by Pharaoh's (12:10–20). This Lord had promised her husband countless descendants (12:2; 13:16; 15:5), but evidently Abraham didn't think she was part of the equation. He was willing to give her up to Pharaoh's harem and later, back in Canaan, to name his slave Eliezer as his heir (15:2, 3). The Lord having vetoed both schemes, she stepped in with a plan of her own.

As a surrogate mother, her maid Hagar was supposed to place the newborn baby on Sarah's knees and then quietly go away. That's how it was done back in Babylonia, at any rate. But to Sarah's horror, her magnanimous scheme backfired (chap. 16). Hagar made fun of her, kept the boy Ishmael for herself, and got blessed by the Lord in spite of it all!

What Sarah didn't know was that the Lord had her in mind all along.

"I will bless her, and she shall give rise to nations; kings of peoples shall come from her" (17:16). When he heard this, Abraham fell down laughing. The Lord continued: Sarah will indeed have a son; the everlasting covenant will be established through Sarah, with *her* son (17:19). While the narrator made the promise clear, evidently Abraham brushed it off as absurd. He picked himself up, circumcised Ishmael, and decided not to bother Sarah with the subject. Surely he must have heard wrong . . .

Entertaining Angels Unaware

Perhaps he is still thinking it over when the strangers arrive. While the narrator knows this is really a theophany, a visit from the Lord (18:1, 9–15), Sarah and Abraham do not. What they see are simply "three men" (18:2–8, 16). From inside the tent Sarah hears her husband bustling about with a Near Eastern show of hospitality. He greets the travelers, bowing low, and with great understatement offers a little bread and water. Then he hastens to prepare a feast. The tent-flap flies open: Psst! Sarah! Knead the flour and make some cakes! Amused, she shakes her head. Whoever heard of rushing yeast? Even in this heat the bread takes hours to rise.

She is still waiting for the yeast to do its work as the three men finish their breadless feast. She overhears them ask Abraham her whereabouts. How did these strangers know her name? Now she listens hard at the tent entrance. Her hearing is still good, even at ninety. What follows is the oddest announcement: "Your wife Sarah will have a son" (v. 10). What's going on here? First Abraham wants instant bread, now a total stranger predicts a postmenopausal birth! And so, quite naturally, she laughs.

The laughter elicits questions from the stranger, whom both Sarah and Abraham recognize now to be the Lord. "Why did Sarah laugh . . . ? Is anything too wonderful for the LORD?" (18:13, 14) The questions are genuine and open-ended rather than rhetorical. The Lord means to continue the conversation. New possibilities exist; a son is waiting to be born. "No, I didn't laugh," Sarah says. Is the news too good to be true? Is it perhaps too good not to be true? Lest her laughter foreclose the possibility, even as absurd a possibility as this, she denies it.

But the Lord let her laughter be. "Oh yes, you did laugh." And the child will be called just that: Isaac, which means

> "For nothing will be impossible with God." This story resonates with the annunciation to Mary in Luke 1:37.

"laughter." Far from judging her response, the Lord joins in the mirth. God recognizes the quirkiness of the equation: barren womb plus elderly woman equals new mother. And so it is, a year later, that the birth of Isaac is told in 21:1–7. We can imagine the aged parents with their healthy baby boy, playing peekaboo and looking marvelously foolish. It's an odd, knee-slapping, glorious moment. Sarah says, "God has brought laughter for me; everyone who hears will laugh with me" (21:6). Such a thing just can't happen, can it? Is anything too wonderful for the Lord?

Making All Things New

Our culture is obsessed with the new. Consumerism feeds the obsession; we are caught in a vicious cycle as we seek out new entertainment, new bodies, new attitudes, and always more prestige and money. "You can't be too rich or too thin," consumer culture tells women, and the sorry truism breeds cosmetic surgery and anorexic teenagers. "You can't be too powerful or too virile," our culture tells men, while Viagra pills fly off the shelves and some athletes are paid more each year than some third-world nations' annual budget.

Our culture seeks renewal.

It's an age of bread and circuses, but the newness we seek leaves us starving for more stuff, bigger thrills. This is because consumer ideology is an idolatry that promises much, but delivers nothing. We settle for half-truths because the truth of God's newness seems too outrageous, too wonderful. We settle for a closed system where hopes are constantly recycled but no real surprise is possible. God as the source of all things new spells death to our cherished idolatries. That death is the one thing our culture simply will not afford.

But the question is put to Sarah and Abraham: Is anything too wonderful for the Lord? Startling possibilities were being announced to them. Absurd, maybe. Peculiar, certainly. But "laughter" (Isaac) opened up a closed, fixed system. Yes, there is something new under the sun. "See, I am making all things new" (Rev. 21:5). God will always find a way into the future. This is gospel, good news, indeed.

> "Faith is a scandal. The promise is beyond our expectation and beyond all evidence. The 'impossibility possibility' of God deals frighteningly with our future."—Walter Brueggemann, *Genesis*, Interpretation, 162.

The Evils of Sodom

The strangers take their leave in 18:16, setting out for Sodom with Abraham in attendance. As Sarah overheard the conversation earlier, Abraham now overhears a remarkable theological reflection. It is God thinking things over.

Years ago, after their return from Egypt, Abraham had made his nephew Lot an offer (13:2–13). Between the two of them there was too much stuff: possessions, flocks, herds, tents. If they separated they could divide the land and keep the peace. Abraham gave Lot first pick; Lot chose the fertile plain of the Jordan River valley and left his uncle with the scrubby highlands. Lot himself settled in Sodom, known to be a city of wickedness.

Whatever legal definitions exist for "sodomy" today, they have nothing to do with the evils of Sodom described by the prophets. "This was the guilt of your sister Sodom: she and her daughters had pride, excess of food, and prosperous ease, but did not aid the poor and needy" (Ezek. 16:49). Unlike Abraham, the citizens of Sodom were unable to show hospitality to strangers (see Luke 10:8–12). It is not homosexual activity that is described in 19:4, 5, but rather gang rape, which is always an act of violence.

The Lord has made a preliminary judgment against Sodom in 18:20. But the Lord has also made a commitment to Abraham. Abraham is "chosen," the first installation in a great design to bring righteousness and justice throughout the earth. The Lord has made Abraham part of the master plan. Now, as Abraham overhears, the Lord ponders whether Abraham should be privy to the preliminary plan concerning Sodom.

Abraham Questions God

The "way of the Lord" is what God chose Abraham to teach the next generation. It is the way of righteousness and justice (v. 19). But what might this mean? In the generation of Noah, this way meant a narrow focus on one family, remembered by God and saved from the flood. In Genesis 19 this convention is repeated, on a smaller scale, as God remembers Abraham (19:29) and saves Lot's family from the seismic explosion. The calculus is simple, serious, and fatal. The way of wickedness is death; further, wickedness has the power to carry all, with the exception of one family, off the face of the earth. If Genesis 19 is taken alone, the "way of the LORD" is a simple teaching of retribution. The destruction of

> "The story . . . is structured to show the tension between the *faith of Abraham* and the *waywardness of humanity*."—Walter Brueggemann, *Genesis*, Interpretation, 163.

Sodom tells us nothing new. But Abraham speaks and drives a wedge through retribution theology. Abraham opens the heart of God.

In 18:25 Abraham clears his throat, then puts a bold question to the Lord: "Shall not the Judge of all the earth do what is just?" Does God's justice predispose God toward punishment? If we humans are to teach "the way of the Lord," and that way is judgment, then who will be left to teach? Abraham, God's confidant, offers up a new possibility. He asks God to consider a different way. Heretofore, God's justice meant that wickedness outweighed goodness in the divine scales. Why not have it otherwise? Why not allow the righteous more weight? Who has priority in the heart of God?

In 18:23–33, Abraham questions the conventional formula. Will the righteous be carried off with the wicked? Will evil finally have power over good? It is ancient Near Eastern bargaining at its best. With tact, Abraham starts the haggling at fifty righteous. To Abraham's surprise, God agrees. Perhaps God is surprised too. The Lord receives Abraham's questions with interest and hospitality. There is no little humor in all this as Abraham rapidly shifts from pointed questions to bickering to deference and back again. Forty-five? Forty? Thirty? Twenty? Each time the response comes back: For the sake of these few, the Lord will not destroy the city. The negotiations stop at ten.

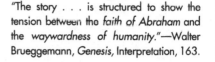

Want to Know More?

About laughter in the Bible? See Paul J. Achtemeier, *Harper's Bible Dictionary* (San Francisco: Harper & Row, 1985), 547–48; about the use of humor in scripture, see Douglas Adams, *The Prostitute in the Family Tree: Discovering Humor and Irony in the Bible* (Louisville, Ky.: Westminster John Knox Press, 1997); about finding the humorous in daily life, see J. Marshall Jenkins, *The Ancient Laugh of God: Divine Encounters in Unlikely Places* (Louisville, Ky.: Westminster John Knox Press, 1994).

About the sin of Sodom? See Walter Brueggemann, *Genesis*, Interpretation, 164. For a thorough but technical discussion, see Brian Doyle, "The Sin of Sodom: *yada', yada', yada'*? A Reading of the Mamre-Sodom Narrative in Genesis 18–19," *Theology and Sexuality*, no. 9 (September 1998): 84–100; Doyle downplays the sexual overtones to suggest that the sin is the Sodomite's *pride* in trying to know God by force.

There is nothing fixed about the number ten; the postulate is radically new and therefore open-ended. His intercession makes a difference. And now, in the heart of God, a new righteousness is made possible. In Isaiah 53:5, 10, vicarious righteousness is conceived for the many by one servant who suffers. In the New Testament, righteousness is made available to all because of the crucified Christ. Jesus is the one who takes the power of sin and death into his own person, and explodes them, like the seismic overthrow of Sodom, from within. God's will to save has more power than the greatest evil, and predominates over God's will to judge.

Show Hospitality

Abraham's intercession is bold and persistent. What enables him to enter into this process? What moves him to break open new possibilities for the Lord in dealing with the world? His credentials are extraordinary. He is chosen by God to keep the way of justice and righteousness. He will become a great nation and all the earth will be blessed through him. With qualifications like this, Abraham has unique authority. His pointed questions to God are reflected in Jeremiah, Job, the Psalms, Habakkuk. His intercession carries weight and sets an example for Moses (Ex. 32:11–14) and Amos (Amos 7:1–6).

We do not share the credentials of Abraham, but we do share his humanness. What he has, and what God listens to, is his compassion for the stranger. He shows hospitality (Greek *philoxenia,* love of strangers; compare Heb. 13:2) in 18:1–8. He demonstrates concern for a city, and a wicked one at that, in 18:22–33. He could simply have asked for the removal of Lot from the disaster. Instead he asks God to spare the entire city, a city of strangers, for the sake of the righteous.

We are told in 19:4 that all of Sodom's men, young and old, threatened the angelic strangers. It is a conventional formula for judgment. Any moral code would call for quick destruction, which is what happens. All are guilty, therefore all are doomed. But Abraham urges: What if? What if the blanket statement of 19:4, like any stereotype, does not cover every person in Sodom? What if the other half of the population (women) and children are considered too? What if, as Jesus later urges, even our enemies are to be the subjects of our prayers (Matt. 5:44)?

Violent and profane, Sodom's men are today's strangers whom we fear. We shun them in the darkness of night, and we keep them out of our homes and neighborhoods. "Be careful! Watch out for strangers," we tell our children, and we take care to surround ourselves with folks like us. Xenophobia comes naturally to us, while *philoxenia* (love of the stranger) seems absurd.

Yet it was a stranger who brought the news to Abraham and Sarah. And on the road to Emmaus, a stranger brought two dispirited apostles news of the resurrected Christ, who was himself the stranger (Luke 24:13–35). The stranger provides us an uncommon opportunity. "I was a stranger and you welcomed me," the Son of Man says (Matt. 25:35). Asked by the righteous when such a thing occurred, he replies, "As you did it to one of the least of these . . . you did it to me" (25:40).

The writer of Hebrews says, "Do not neglect to show hospitality to strangers, for by doing that some have entertained angels without knowing it" (13:2). Who of us knows what gift the stranger might bring? Quaker theologian Parker

Today we are afraid of strangers.

Palmer offers a definition: "The stranger is a bearer of truth which might not otherwise have been received" (Palmer, 58). Abraham knew this, and when we venture out into the world of strangers we learn it too.

The role of the stranger in our lives is vital in the context of the Christian faith, for the God of faith is one who continually speaks truth afresh, who continually makes all things new. God persistently challenges conventional truth and regularly upsets the world's way of looking at things. It is no accident that this is so often represented by the stranger, for the truth that God speaks in our lives is very strange indeed. Where the world sees impossibility, God sees potential. Where the world sees comfort, God sees idolatry. Where the world sees insecurity, God sees occasions for faith. Where the world sees death, God proclaims life. God uses the stranger to shake us from our conventional points of view, to remove the scales of worldly assumptions from our eyes. (Palmer, 59)

> "Faith is laughter at the promise of a child called laughter."—Frederick Buechner, *Wishful Thinking: A Theological ABC* (New York: Harper & Row, 1973), 25.

We open up our hands and the startled baby laughs. The diptych of Genesis 18 opens up and startles us with glimpses of laughter and good news, of hospitality and concern. In God there are new possibilities. They come to us in the strangest of ways.

 Questions for Reflection

1. "Is anything too wonderful for the Lord?" Time and again, the presence or promise of God is revealed in scripture in the birth of a child. What are some of the other special births in the Bible? (Use a concordance if necessary.)
2. Sarah laughs at what seems preposterous news. What might your response have been in the same circumstances? Why?
3. Abraham negotiates with God as did Cain and as will Moses. What are the terms of Abraham's negotiations? These three examples suggest that humans (of any rank or standing) *can* negotiate with God. What do you think?
4. This unit refers to strangers who bear "truth which might not otherwise have been received." What is your normal response to strangers? Are there strangers who bear truth in your life? Who might they be?

The Testing of Abraham

"Take your son, your only son . . . whom you love, and . . . offer him . . . as a burnt offering."

Imagine an audience of children, dressed in their Sunday best and crowded around little tables in the classroom. It's church school and they are eager, as young children are, to please their teacher, who is you. And your assignment this morning is to tell them the Genesis 22 story. You aren't even sure what to call it: The testing of Abraham? The sacrifice of Isaac? The strange demands of God? Your task is daunting.

Perhaps you can get this over with quickly, without too many questions, and fill up the rest of the Sunday school hour with snack time, maybe some indoor games. Perhaps the children will *not* be so attentive today. It has happened before. So you launch right in with an eye on the clock. You clear your throat, and begin . . .

Abraham took his son Isaac where he was told, as God commanded. When they got to the mountaintop, Abraham built an altar, which was used back then as a place for worshiping God with animal sacrifices (we don't do this today). At the last minute an angel stopped him. He sacrificed a ram, which is a boy sheep, on the altar. God was happy and they all got to go back home.

The children sit quiet, puzzled. One little boy raises his hand and asks, "How old was Isaac?" You aren't sure—the text doesn't say—but you know that for these children the boy Isaac is exactly their age. Another hand comes up: "Why did God want the father to kill anyone, especially his own son?" You glance at the laminated poster of the Ten Commandments on the wall and clear your throat again. "Well, Abraham didn't kill Isaac now, did he? God didn't want that."

And then the new girl, the shy one who observes everything but says little, murmurs: "I wonder what Isaac was thinking." It's so quiet the class overhears her. They wonder now, too, because what if that wasn't Isaac long ago, but them today? What if God told Daddy or Mama to kill them? What if Daddy or Mama actually would?

> "Throughout human history, children have been used, against their will, in adults' attempts to satisfy or placate their gods."— Donald Capps, *The Child's Song: The Religious Abuse of Children* (Louisville, Ky.: Westminster John Knox Press, 1995), 78.

Next year, you vow, if there is a next year, you will skip this lesson in Sunday school.

A Disturbing Passage

Because the passage is so difficult and so many interpretive decisions must be made, we will limit ourselves to two tasks. First we will look closely at the structure of the text itself, allowing the text to say what it has to say to us. Second we will look to other voices in the biblical canon. Genesis 22, while it is a unique text, does not stand alone. We can bring in other passages to stand next to it, speak to it, and speak to us in our perplexity.

The passage is structured with symmetry and artistry. An emphatic summons is issued three times: "Abraham!" (v. 1); "Father!" (v. 7); "Abraham, Abraham!" (v. 11). The response to each call is the same: "Here I am." Throughout the episode Abraham is grounded in his reply and ready to act.

> The Hebrew word for "burnt sacrifice" (v. 2, NRSV) connotes a sacrifice consumed by fire, which is the definition of our English word "holocaust."

The first call is from God, who gives the chilling command (v. 2). It is not simply Isaac, but "your only son, whom you love" who is the object of the command. It is a careful and excruciating description: Not that one, not the one you don't like, but this one, Isaac, who is yours alone. Isaac is to be offered up to God at a faraway place, three days' journey from Beersheba. The land of Moriah is unknown; in 2 Chronicles 3:1 the mountain is identified with Jerusalem. The place is known only to God, who will show Abraham where to make the sacrifice.

The events of verse 3 are told with no emotional content whatsoever. We are given no insight as to Abraham's state of mind. Instead we have a terse picture of father Abraham simply performing the necessary tasks: rising early, saddling the donkey, cutting the wood, taking Isaac and two servants with him. The wooden description matches his automatic movements. He speaks to no one. The dark command is dumbfounding.

The journey is reported without commentary. All we know is there are three days, but days of what? Grim resignation? Reflection? Silence? Tears? Idle chatter? In such a crisis, what does one say to one's son? To God? The hiatus is a mystery. Yet we know that, when the third day arrives, Abraham is able to speak with authority. He leaves his servants behind with instructions and an agenda.

God Will Provide

While the servants are to wait, he and Isaac will go off to worship and then they, father and son, will return: "We will come back to you" (v. 5). Given verse 2, this assurance is extraordinary. On one hand Abraham does not want the servants to witness the sacrifice; on the other hand he witnesses to them of his son's safekeeping and homecoming. There is no hint of duplicity in his language either here or elsewhere in the passage. He is able with confidence to speak of the future.

They trudge along, Isaac carrying the wood while Abraham carries the fire and the knife. Isaac's age is not given, but he is old enough to tote wood to make an altar, and to know what their mission is. He calls "Father!" and asks the whereabouts of the lamb, given all the other implements for a burnt offering. It is the

> ". . . in our present text, unexpected things happen. Only now do we see how serious faith is. This narrative shows that we do not have a tale of origins, but a story of anguished faith."—Walter Brueggemann, *Genesis*, Interpretation, 185.

second time Abraham has been summoned. It is the only time he answers both with action and with speech.

He stops and says to his son, "God himself will provide the lamb for a burnt offering" (v. 8). This is the key verse of the narrative. It is simple and direct. There is God, there is to be a burnt offering, and there will be a lamb. The verb "provide" is the indispensable action.

"Provide" is an unusual translation of the Hebrew "to see." The sense is best rendered as the Latin *pro-video:* to see before, to see to, to see about. In spite of the dark demand, God himself will see to it. Providence means just this. Abraham trusts that the inscrutable test (v. 1) is not the last word. God will see to that. Isaac looks to his father, and Abraham looks to God.

Abraham's response, given in this decisive verse 8, comes from deep inside the mystery of faith. His words are the only appropriate words to give to his son, because they are true. He is not a man of blind obedience or passivity. He is a person who trusts. As his son trusts in him, so Abraham trusts in God. The assurance of the son is paralleled in the assurance of the father. "So the two of them walked on together." Abraham's actions mirror his speech. Together they will go and see how God will provide.

The Sacrifice Is Prepared

Because we are heartened by Abraham's words in verses 5 and 8, we are not prepared for the ominous undertaking on the mountaintop. Father and son arrive at the place God has shown. With verse 9, the terse narration of automatic action resumes. Grimly Abraham assembles the altar. Carefully he stacks the wood for the pyre. Silently Isaac is bound for slaughter and laid on the wood. He will soon become the burnt offering. The horror of the scene peaks as Abraham reaches out to take the knife (v. 10).

Is he to drive a knife through his own son, the child of the promise and his old age? Is he to kill another human being? Is he to slaughter the boy with a bloody knife, like an animal? Can there be anything more terrible?

> "This is Hebrew story-telling at its masterly best. It is not the kind of story-telling we are used to from modern writers, but even across the centuries and in English translation it can grip us so that the knuckles of our clenched hands show white, and move us to the most intense of emotions."—John C. L. Gibson, *Genesis*, vol. 2, Daily Study Bible (Philadelphia: Westminster Press, 1982), 112.

The angel, which is the voice of God, calls him at this perilous moment. It is a wonder that Abraham can hear at all, with the blood pounding through his ears and the thought of his son's blood pouring over the pyre. For the third time he answers, "Here I am." He is told to stop; this second command overrides the first. "Don't touch him!" Looking up, he sees that a ram is caught in a thicket. This is the creature provided him by God.

The ram is sacrificed and burned. The narrator makes it clear that it was to be either the child of God's promise or the ram of God's pro-

viding. Abraham "offered it up as a burnt offering instead of his son" (v. 13). He is still to worship, as commanded in verse 2. But his sacrifice was made just before. As the voice says, "You have not withheld your son, your only son, from me." In the response to God's in-scrutable demand, Abraham has with-held nothing, not even the son he loves. Gladly would he have given his own life instead. But this was not commanded.

"The LORD will provide . . ."

Put to the Test

Does Abraham fear God? The test, as in the book of Job, is a real one. No one knows for sure. The future is open-ended and the results cannot be deter-mined beforehand. Between the command of verse 2 ("Take your son and go") and the second command of verse 12 ("Do not do anything to him"), real awareness happens and real movement occurs. God did not know what Abraham would do; God says, "Now I know." And with this knowledge comes action. God swears an oath (v. 16) binding God to the promise.

Abraham will become a mighty nation, his offspring will possess the land, and through him all the nations of the earth will be blessed (vv. 17, 18). The threefold promise stands, with Isaac still its heir (see 21:12). The drama is over and the crisis is resolved.

In a very important sense, this text is unique in the biblical canon. Only in the book of Job do we find such testing of an individual by God, testing of such momentous and terrible proportions.

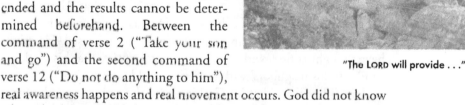

"To assert that God *provides* requires a faith as intense as does the conviction that God *tests*."—Walter Brueggemann, *Genesis*, Interpretation, 191.

Like Abraham, Job is a friend of God. He too is prepared to trust the God who gives and the God who takes away (Job 1:21). Job's poetry asks about faith: the tension between the cost and the joy of faithfulness. He feels the cost acutely in both the presence of his friends and the absence of God. But his test differs from Abraham's. Job's children are taken from him but not by his own hand. Nowhere is Job commanded to slaughter his own.

While God permits the testing of Job, the torment is inflicted by Satan. In a sense the testing is indirect; this was Satan's idea. What does the canon say about the direct testing of God's people?

First off, nowhere is child sacrifice condoned in the Bible. Pagan worshipers made human sacrifices to propitiate the gods, especially the god Molech in Moabite rites. In contrast to their pagan neighbors, such sacrifice was abhorrent to Israel (Lev. 18:21; 20:2–5). Israel was certainly guilty of mimicking the surrounding nations, and of offering human sacrifice in dire straits (cf. Jer 7:31; 32:35). For this they were condemned. God does not test in this way, with the important exception of Abraham.

> "The story of the near-sacrifice of Isaac may rest upon a rather common and widespread motif in which a hero, often at the command of a deity, is forced to sacrifice his own son or daughter."—John Van Seters, *Prologue to History: The Yahwist as Historian in Genesis* (Louisville, Ky.: Westminster John Knox Press, 1992), 261.

One might argue that Abraham, of course, did not know the Levitical law. He was of pagan stock; his was a world littered with pagan gods who must be appeased. He might have thought at first, with dismay but not surprise, that his God was similar to his neighbors' with respect to child sacrifice.

The difference is that his God initiated the action, not Abraham. And more importantly, both the narrator and the reader know the horror of the command. Indeed the absurdity is the very point. This God was bound to Abraham in promise; now the child of promise is to be bound and slain. Who is this strange God? The biblical record affirms that this is a God who tests.

Testing and Providing

The testing of God is known in the wilderness wanderings. "[God] fed you in the wilderness with manna that your ancestors did not know, to humble you and to test you, and in the end to do you good"

(Deut. 8:16). There are important parallels between the teaching in Deuteronomy and the testing of Abraham. Both Abraham and the Israelite nation are "new" to God. In both cases God wants to "know" their hearts (cf. Deut. 8:2). God provides for Abraham with the ram, and for the Israelites with the manna. Genuine movement occurs in each narrative. God moves the promise into the future with Isaac. God moves the Israelites into the promised land. The same God who tests is the one who does good in the end.

The testing/tempting of God is also known in the Lord's Prayer. "Lead us not into temptation," Jesus instructs us to ask (Matt. 6:13; Luke 11:4). We are praying that God spare us tests we cannot bear: the test of Abraham on Mount Moriah, or of forty years wandering in the desert. Few of us

> ### 📖 Want to Know More?
>
> **About providence?** See Shirley C. Guthrie, *Christian Doctrine*, revised ed. (Louisville, Ky.: Westminster John Knox Press, 1994), 166–91; Daniel L. Migliore, *The Power of God* (Philadelphia: Westminster Press, 1983), 80–90.
>
> **About child sacrifices in ancient times?** See George Arthur Buttrick, *The Interpreter's Dictionary of the Bible*, vol. R–Z (Nashville: Abingdon Press, 1962), 153–54.
>
> **About suffering and the Jewish faith?** See Stephen R. Haynes, *Reluctant Witnesses: Jews and the Christian Imagination* (Louisville, Ky.: Westminster John Knox Press, 1995).

could respond as Abraham did. Even fewer are asked to obey the dark command, for it would drive us to despair. But the Lord's Prayer likewise links the God who tests with the God who provides. We can ask with assurance for bread, the daily ration of manna, trusting that God will see to it. The same God who makes inscrutable tests is known in gracious providing. The Lord's Prayer holds this tension together, whether we are fully aware of it or not as we pray.

Faith, the Assurance of Things Hoped For

The human tendency is to break this tension. Either God tests or God provides, but not both. In bitterness and despair, those without hope see only the God who tests. In complacency and self-satisfaction, those who feel blessed see only the God who provides. This God is a great cosmic vending machine who spits out the good life in exchange for our tokens. It is a level-headed, businesslike, rational approach to religion which makes God a player in a market economy.

But faith is not a business deal. It is not a means to an end. The hard work of faith is to embrace the tension. And this is what Abraham does at Moriah. This is what Jesus does at Gethsemane (Mark 14:36).

Finally, Genesis 22 cannot be separated from an earlier narrative, the call of Abraham in Genesis 12. In the movement from providing to testing and back again, the two episodes stand as brackets around a long, eventful life. Abraham's faithfulness works itself out in a variety of ways. Elsewhere he raises questions and objections to God's plan (18:22–33). In the bracketing episodes, Abraham is silent.

The Abraham cycle begins and ends with the threefold promise. The oath of 22:17, 18 echoes what God promised in 12:2, 3. God's

promise to Abraham does not change; instead it is renewed and emphasized. Genesis 22 brings the narrative to a dramatic and perplexing resolution. This marks the last time God speaks to Abraham. We might wish it to end differently, but it does not.

The connections between Genesis 22 and Genesis 12 are many. In a Hebrew construction unique in the Old Testament, God says in effect: "Get going" (12:2; 22:2). God calls Abraham to take leave of the most important thing: the land of his father (12:1), the child of his old age (22:2, compare 21:2). In both cases God's command is mysterious, enigmatic, impenetrable. The ultimate destination is withheld. Nevertheless, although he is silent, Abraham's response is full and immediate (12:4; 22:3). Both episodes show the great courage of Abraham, which is based purely on his faith.

As you pass out the juice and cookies, you overhear three of the children talking. "Hey. Didn't God have a son? Didn't God give up Jesus on the cross?"

"Yeah, but you know how *that* ended. He got raised from the dead!"

"Yeah! I can't wait till Easter! Hey, you want that cookie?" You grin and ruffle his hair. And you decide you just might make it as a Sunday school teacher, after all.

Questions for Reflection

1. This may be the most troubling passage in scripture. Yet it remains, and Abraham is applauded as a shining example of faith. What would you have done if you were in Abraham's predicament? Why has this troubling story remained a part of our religious tradition?

2. What do we mean when we talk about the providence of God? Does God know or cause everything that happens? Why or why not?

3. If you had to present this story to a children's Sunday school class, how would you tell it? How would you answer their questions?

4. Some see this story as support for the belief that sometimes God calls individuals (or whole nations) to be a witness, and that being a witness may include suffering or sacrifice. How do you respond to that belief?

8 Genesis 28:10–22

Jacob's Dream at Bethel

Ever wanted to get away from it all? Our culture tells us that we can get the right car or a credit card and do just that. We can drive off into the sunset or fly across continents; we can charge wonderful exotic things and hang out with handsome and beautiful people. In our consumer culture, a new life can be bought. Get away, find yourself, and never mind the bills or the past. The old can be left behind like a cicada's shell on a tree.

Jacob had plenty to get away from. As the scene opens in 28:10, Jacob's brother and father are both victims of his guile (chap. 27). While his father, Isaac, has sent him off with a blessing (28:3), Jacob has nevertheless been sent off, to Paddan-aram, four hundred miles from home. His twin Esau hates him and wishes him dead (27:41). Rebekah planned a sort of witness relocation program for her favorite son, convincing Isaac that Jacob will find a suitable wife back in her ancestral land (27:46). Jacob will get away from it all.

Whether he knows it or not, Jacob is at the lowest point in his life. He has betrayed his father and made an enemy of his brother. He has coveted and absconded with the birthright, which gives him the double share of the inheritance (25:29–34), and the blessing, giving him privilege and prosperity (27:28, 29). He has the latest model luxury sedan and the gold credit card. But he is a fugitive, and he travels alone.

However, we know from the start that Jacob is special. He is the answer to prayer

> "Jacob was on his way, a long meandering way, to becoming Israel." H. Stephen Shoemaker, *GodStories: New Narratives from Sacred Texts* (Valley Forge, Pa.: Judson Press, 1998), 53.

for a barren couple (25:21). The Lord gives him preeminence over his twin, who was born first (25:23). (The oracle of 25:23 is given to Rebekah, who subsequently loves Jacob best.) But the only time Jacob invokes the Lord is in the ruse of 27:10, when he lies to his father. The episode of 28:10–22 marks the first encounter between Jacob and God.

The Things Dreams Are Made Of

It is important to note that the encounter is both a visual experience and a speech. The visual elements are striking and memorable, but what Jacob *sees* merely sets the stage for what is central. The *word* of promise is what the scene is all about. The speech of God, then, is our focal point.

The theophany occurs in a dream, that state of mind in which humans have no control. The dream state is the domain God chose to reveal God's self. We are familiar today with dreams as psychological phenomena. We might wish to dismiss the theophany and say that Jacob's unconscious desires were being manifest in his dream state, or look at the visual elements as archetypes and symbols. But the text will not allow us to deny the objective reality of the dream. The dream does not stand for anything; it is what it is.

Keep in mind that Jacob has never been less "worthy" of a theophany than he is at this time. He did not seek out the Lord. He did not merit the promises. Jacob is a conflicted man whose chief concern is survival. He is on the road, fleeing his past, and this particular night he is in no particular place. Exiled and threatened, the last thing he would expect is the word that comes to him in the night.

> "The element in the narrative that surprises Jacob and seems incredible to us is not the religious phenomenon of appearance. It is the wonder, mystery, and shock that this God should be present in such a decisive way to this exiled one."— Walter Brueggemann, *Genesis*, Interpretation, 242.

Yet Jacob is sure that God spoke to him there (28:16). What startles Jacob, and us, is not that God spoke, but that God chose this time to speak to one who was treacherous, deceptive, and unworthy of the speech. God is bound to Jacob. God makes outrageous and unconditional promises to a person and changes the course of history in doing so. Such is the character of God.

God's Promise

The news is a blessing that makes the future possible for Jacob. Verse 15 is addressed specifically to Jacob; it is on this key verse that we will focus. But just prior to the announcement that is unique to Jacob, verses 13–14 repeat the threefold promise first issued to Abraham in 12:1–3 and reissued in 26:4 to Isaac. The patriarchs and matriarchs of Genesis are told that (1) they will become a mighty nation, (2) they will inherit the land of promise, and (3) all the nations of the earth will be blessed through them. God has sworn that it will be so; God has *limited* God's power in a way that binds God to these promises. The divine options are no longer so open-ended. This binding of God to a particular people is the meaning of covenant and the heart of the good news in the Genesis stories.

While the first two parts of the promise focus on the well-being of this particular people (descendants, land), the last concerns the well-being of others (12:3; 18:18; 22:18; 26:4). God is indeed interested in this people, but they are not to retreat into self-interest. God moves them beyond narrow concerns. The way in which this people is to become a blessing to the world is not developed in Genesis; it is Isaiah who will pick up this theme and magnify it. For now, this part of the promise is implicit, hidden, undeveloped.

> "This promise presents a central thrust of biblical faith. It refutes all the despairing judgments about human existence. A fresh understanding of God is required if we are to be delivered from the hopeless analyses of human possibility made by pessimistic scientists and by the poets of existence."—Walter Brueggemann, *Genesis*, Interpretation, 244–45.

The hint that Jacob should be the heir to this promise is given at his birth (25:23). No reason is given for this choice, just as none was given to his grandfather Abraham. Jacob is given priority over Esau, who is imminently more likable and good. It is the inscrutable will of God that a nomad from Ur of the Chaldees would receive this word and that his deceptive, scheming grandson would as well.

The threefold promise of verse 15 is addressed specifically to Jacob. "I am with you." "I will keep you." "I will bring you back." The promise involves God's presence, God's action, and Jacob's homecoming.

God with Us

"I am with you." The visual elements of the dream correspond to these words. The ladder, or better, "ramp," is borrowed from ancient Near Eastern religious iconography. Mesopotamian ziggurats were temples formed like stacked building blocks making stairways or ramps to the heavens. The gods were "up there" and it was the worshiper's task to ascend to them. The stairway provided the means of approach to the gods, the link from the human sphere upward to the divine. But the ramp in Genesis 28:12 is God's doing. Heaven meets earth because God has decided it would be so. While the ancient world conceived the movement in one way, from the bottom up, the good news is that here we find God bridging the gap. "The LORD stood beside him" (v. 13); God speaks directly to him. Indeed, the gap does not exist at all.

Eighteenth-century Deism pictured God as the Great Watchmaker who created the great clock of the universe, wound it up, and hurled it out to tick away with its own scientific laws and rhythms. God might be an interested bystander, but such a God would not interfere with creation, indeed could not change it. While the Deists might offer thanks to this God for the gift of creation, intercessory prayer was unthinkable. God had simply stepped out of the picture.

The ramp and the promise shatter this theology. Jacob is not alone. Earth cannot be divorced from the presence of God. The biblical record agrees with the Deists' conception of the creator God, but it goes further than that. God does not create and then leave creation to its own devices any more than a mother gives birth and leaves the baby at the doorstep. God is both creator and sustainer, life giver and nurturer. "You are always mine" is the implied promise to the exiled Cain as he is given the mark of God's protection (Gen. 4:15). It is the promise to Jeremiah as he is called to the terrifying office of the prophet (Jer. 1:19). It is the word given to the exiled community in Babylon (Isa. 43:1, 2). Finally, it is the name of Jesus: "Emmanuel," God with us (Matt. 1:23; see also John 1:51).

Upheld by My Hand

"I will keep you." The visual element that corresponds to these words is the presence of the angels in verse 12 (see also 32:1, 2). The world is upheld, sustained, kept by God. Israel is graven in the palm of God's hand (Isa. 49:16); we are supported from underneath by the everlasting arms (Deut. 33:27, RSV).

A favorite picture of God in both the Old Testament and the New Testament is the shepherd. As the shepherd is the keeper of the flock, so God is the keeper of Jacob. Sheep require a lot of overseeing. They are obstinate and stubborn, panicky and defenseless. They butt heads to establish a hierarchy in the herd. They can starve to death just yards away from good pastureland but return time and again to polluted watering holes. When they get fat they are easily "cast," flaying frantically and unable to get up unassisted. There is nothing particularly lovable about them. They are, in fact, a pain. And they are, in fact, like us. God keeps the flock safe, knowing that the job is not a pleasant one and we are bound to make it difficult.

Want to Know More?

About theophanies? See Paul J. Achtemeier, ed., *Harper's Bible Dictionary* (San Francisco: Harper & Row, 1985), 1062–63; Walther Eichrodt, *Theology of the Old Testament*, vol. 2, Old Testament Library (Philadelphia: Westminster Press, 1967), 15–45.

About dreams in the Bible? See Lois Lindsey Hendricks, *Discovering My Biblical Dream Heritage* (San Jose, Calif.: Resource Publications, 1989). If you are interested in dreams and spirituality, see Morton Kelsey, *Dreams: A Way to Listen to God* (New York: Paulist Press, 1978).

About limits to God's power? See Daniel L. Migliore, *The Power of God*, Library of Living Faith (Philadelphia: Westminster Press, 1983), 70–74, 91–101; for a more academic discussion, see E. Frank Tupper, *A Scandalous Providence: The Jesus Story of the Compassion of God* (Macon, Ga.: Mercer University Press, 1995), 326–31, 358–61.

At Journey's End

"I will bring you home." Jacob's exile was for twenty-one years in Paddan-aram. Judah's exile was for fifty years in Babylon. Our modern experience of exile and displacement appears at times to be permanent, without end. We live in a world of displacement. We respond by "nesting" and accumulating things: a home with a security system, an entertainment center, overstuffed couches, and big, billowy bed linens. Surely we can create a home, fill it with stuff that will keep us safe and relieve our anxieties, relax in spite of our tedium or boredom or exhaustion. Patriarchal history affirms this sense of displacement. "A wandering Aramean was my ancestor" (Deut. 26:5). The people of promise are descendants of this wanderer Abraham. The truth is that, like Jacob, we are not at home. Who makes us lie down in green pastures? Who or what restores our soul? The biblical record affirms that this work is God's doing. "Our hearts are restless till they find rest in thee," Augustine said. As fugitives we look for a pillow and find a stone; we settle for a night in a place with no name. We awake to find that the stony place is actually the house of God ("Bethel"). Homecoming is the work of the Lord.

Jacob Awakes

Now we turn from the spoken word of God to the human response. Of one thing Jacob is sure: "Surely the LORD is in this place" (28:16). God spoke in the night in a dream, and God's presence persists as the day dawns. How does Jacob respond?

Jacob characterizes the experience as "awesome." Rudolf Otto, in his classic *The Idea of the Holy* (1917), writes that the response to the holy is not rational; it is beyond conceptual expression. Those who experience the Wholly Other are moved to a painful awareness of creatureliness in the face of tremendous mystery (see Isa. 6:5). They experience a profound sense of awe: of being simultaneously repelled by and drawn to the presence of God, dreading this power and yet fascinated by it. Finally, the experience moves them to action (see Isa. 6:8). We see Jacob responding to God in the fashion described by Otto. Overwhelmed by the awesomeness of the Holy One, he cannot be merely an interested spectator. He is drawn into the holiness of God and moved toward change in his own life.

Fear is the most debilitating of diseases. Fright can provoke flight, but it can also make us rigid and passive. One might say that the opposite of fear is authentic action. In verses 16–22, we see that Jacob moves from fear and guilt to a new reality. He moves from fright and flight toward a concrete, genuine vocation.

He rises early, alert and ready. He sets up a pillar and consecrates it with oil, an anointing that sets the stone apart as sacred

Jacob's pillar may have looked like this.

(as in Ex. 40:9–11). He renames the place, which was once called Luz by the Canaanites. It will be a sacred site to which he will return in 35:14 after his sojourn in Paddan-aram, and a site of great importance in the history of Israel. He declares Bethel to be the gate of heaven. The tower of Babel was supposed to be just that (11:1–9), but it became a ruined monument to human pride. This monument is marked by a simple pillar of stone because God, not human achievement, has made it the gateway to heaven.

Next Jacob makes a vow (vv. 20–22). While some commentators gloss over the "If" at the beginning of his vow, this little word is pivotal. What God has promised unconditionally, Jacob turns into a set of conditions. What God has promised in general terms, Jacob makes specific, detailed, and tangible. The simplicity of verse 15 turns into the rather complicated vow of verses 20–22. His vows are authentic responses, perhaps, but to what? Did God require the tithe and the founding of a shrine? When God promised to "keep" Jacob, does Jacob need to remind God that food and clothing are part of this safekeeping? Finally, Jacob declares that if his conditions are met, "then the LORD shall be my God." What if homecoming does not involve peace in his father's house? What if God does not perform as Jacob specifies? While the actions and words of God are consistent with each other, it is the mark of humanity that the same is not true for us. What Jacob *does* here are acts of faith and trust, pointers to a new reality. But his *words* sound like he still wishes to hedge the bet. If God satisfies Jacob's wish list, then he will respond in faithful obedience (disciplined worship, the concrete act of tithe).

> "I will surely give one tenth to you." Jacob follows the example of Abraham (Gen. 14:20) and offers a tithe back to God (Gen. 28:22).

The Journey Is Our Home

A new world of possibility has indeed opened up to Jacob, a world where fear and mistrust give way to promise and assurance. But he is still Jacob, the schemer, whose modus operandi is to bargain and dicker. He will proceed on his journey a changed man in some ways, but he has in no way "arrived." He makes his first, feeble baby steps in the direction of faith. And these tentative steps are, God might say, enough for now.

While he wanted to get away from it all, what Jacob needed was the presence of God. While he was a fugitive on the

> "Part of the lesson was that, luckily for Jacob, God doesn't love people because of who they are but because of who [God] is. *It's on the house* is one way of saying it and *it's by grace* is another."—Frederick Buechner, *Peculiar Treasures: A Biblical Who's Who* (New York: Harper & Row, 1979), 58.

run, he learned that he was the heir to the promise. The journey is an apt metaphor for Jacob. The journey also applies to the character of God. God is on a divine journey with God's people wherever they might go (Psalm 23; Isa. 43:1–2; 46:3–4). Jacob's dream at Bethel gives us this good news: God is known in the traveling, and we do not make the trip alone.

 ## Questions for Reflection

1. This story is about a dream that changed Jacob's life. Many people cannot even remember their dreams. How do dreams affect people's lives?
2. "Surely the LORD is in this place." Jacob marked the place with a monument and made a vow. Have you ever had moments when you came to this realization? What were those moments like? What are the ways people mark these moments?
3. God makes an unqualified promise to Jacob in verses 14–15, and Jacob responds with a conditional vow to God in verses 20–22. What precipitates the difference in the way Jacob and God approach each other? What are ways people approach God today?
4. Psalm 139:7–8 affirms God's presence even in remote places. What does it mean to be "kept by God"?

Genesis 32:22–32

Jacob Wrestles with God

It has been twenty-one years since they last saw each other. It's like a high school reunion, each anticipating what the other will be like, look like. One of them must travel far to get there, having been gone all these years without sending so much as a word back home. The hair's a little thin, nothing to be done there, but those few extra sit-ups in the morning will hold the paunch in place, perhaps. Should he bring the family or make an entrance on his own? Should he arrive in a stretch limousine or the little red sportscar? So many details to attend to! The right impression must be made.

He carefully packs his best blazer, the one with the monogrammed buttons. He has been highly successful, which helps. He stops off at the bank to get a roll of bills which he inserts in his monogrammed money clip. At the reunion dinner party, at the right time, he'll nonchalantly pull the clip out of the blazer pocket and buy a round of drinks at the cash bar. Understatement speaks volumes.

When he left home, it was hurriedly. Jacob had played his last trick at the time, living up to his name of "Supplanter" or "Trickster," and it wasn't until he met up with Laban in Haran that he learned how sharply those tricks could sting. Laban was his mother's brother and, eventually, his father-in-law. Laban made Jacob look like lightweight when it came to deception. He tricked Jacob out of the best years of his life, but when it was time to leave, Jacob won the last round. He left like a thief in the night with two wives (Laban's daughters Leah and Rachel), two maids (also surrogate mothers), eleven sons, one daughter, and much livestock. He is coming home with a huge retinue. The only question, and it is the pressing question, is what to do with the past.

Esau his twin will be waiting for him. Esau's slow mind has had twenty-one years to brood over the many wrongs Ja-cob has done him: tricking him out of the birthright, stealing the blessing. Their checkered past together ended in 27:45. The narrative of chapter 32 picks right up where it left off; for all we know, Esau is still breathing murderous threats against his brother's life.

> "An ancient Jewish proverb states that when a person has a clear conscience, everyone fears him, but when he has a guilty conscience, he fears everyone else."—Page H. Kelley, *Journey to the Land of Promise: Genesis–Deuteronomy* (Macon, Ga.: Smyth & Helwys, 1997), 51.

Jacob's Plan

Jacob is the quintessential pragmatist. While still safely on the other side of the Jabbok River, he devises a series of plans which betray his heightening anxiety. He sends messengers to "my lord" Esau in Seir, a region of Edom, announcing the return (32:4, 5). The messengers report that Esau will indeed meet him along with four hundred men. Surely this means trouble, Jacob thinks, so he divides his huge camp of family, slaves, and livestock into two companies. One group at least will escape destruction (32:8). The stakes are high and Jacob is desperate.

Typically calm and collected, Jacob cannot think his way out of this mess. He is distressed and fearful, and he turns to God in prayer. The prayer of 32:9–12 is impeccable. Jacob identifies the Lord as God of Abraham and Isaac, and the One who sent for him to come back home (31:13). He confesses his unworthiness before God and his fear of Esau. He asks for deliverance, and reminds God of the promise made back at Bethel (28:15). His safety is of course the issue: "You have said, 'I will surely do you good . . . '"

Having thought it over after a good night's sleep, Jacob then makes a fabulous

> "The listener is not invited to know the outcome until the last moment. The brothers have to wait to see how it all would turn out. The listener must wait with the brothers."—Walter Brueggemann, *Genesis*, Interpretation, 263.

gift of over five hundred choice animals: sheep, goats, camels, cattle, donkeys. The servants are instructed to herd them by droves, an amazing menagerie, and to make sure Esau knows this is Jacob's present to him. The point is appeasement (32:20). Jacob knows he has wronged the brother and the situation is urgent. Perhaps the "gift" will buy Esau's favor.

Jacob in Control

Summing up the action of 32:1–21, we see Jacob's scheme as items on a checklist:

> Send messengers.
> Split up the booty.
> Pray about it.
> Send huge present.

In all this activity, Jacob is thoroughly, if not desperately, in control. He has done all that is humanly possible to insure his safety. Calculation and strategy are practical matters, even as they increase his anxiety and his need to manipulate the situation for his own well-being. And his plans are all circuitous, skewed attempts at reconciliation.

Even the commendable prayer is indirect, for the forgiveness he needs from his brother is not mentioned. Worship means first righting the wrongs, then offering up the sacrifices: ". . . at the altar, if you remember that your brother or sister has something against you . . . [go and] first be reconciled to your brother or sister" (Matt. 5:23, 24). Jacob does all the things that need not be done, omitting the one thing that is direct and therefore difficult for him. The most that can be said about his preparations is that they keep him busy.

> "As God has 'snatched' property for Jacob from Laban, so Jacob prays to be 'snatched' from the power of Esau."—Walter Brueggemann, *Genesis*, Interpretation, 265.

We are Jacob. We prognosticate and plan, we strategize and prioritize. We do not ask directly and we avoid that which is uncomfortable. Jacob's fears are his attempt to keep control of the situation. If he frets enough, some magic might occur whereby the danger disappears. Surely our worries are worthy of something! "Hope for the best but plan for the worst" is a cultural motto. It is, we believe, pragmatic advice. And it is spiritually bankrupt.

Losing Control

The good news of the Jacob story is different. The action of Genesis 32 moves back and forth between the secular and the sacred as Jacob prepares to meet his brother. Pragmatic preparation and holy intervention overlap; the practical and the spiritual are intertwined. God does not leave Jacob alone, the sole master of his worries. Instead, God appears to him, at night, and wrestles him to the ground.

This is disturbing to us; we cannot imagine how frightening it is to Jacob. It is not a quick and easy solution. The wrestling match is inhumanly lengthy, brutally painful. God will not be left out of the equation; God will terrify Jacob. While Jacob would prefer a hearty slap on the back, the mysterious one grants him a wrenching experience that leaves him limping. Jacob could not in his wildest dreams anticipate this wrestling match, work out a little harder at the gym and build up his strength for it. It comes to him out of nowhere and directly. If he had to choose between meeting Esau and meeting God, surely he would chose the former. But for once, Jacob has no control.

An Unexpected Assailant

Genesis 32:22–32 is one of those key texts in the Old Testament. Shrouded in mystery and ambiguity, it has been retold and examined perhaps more than any other of the patriarchal materials. Moses too meets up with a dreadful presence, also at night and on his way back home (Ex. 4:24). It is an archaic story of a killer angel whose meaning escapes us, except as an explanation for circumcision (already better explained in Gen. 17:10–14). The story of Jacob and the dark presence is likewise an ancient one. But placed where it is, between his practical plans and the meeting with Esau, it takes on a whole new significance. We don't hear many sermons about the Moses episode. This passage, in contrast, is pivotal.

Jacob is alone in the night. He has (again shrewdly) sent the women and children on, across the Jabbok River, far ahead of him (32:22, 23). Not even Esau at his angriest could attack these defenseless ones; besides, Jacob himself is safely far behind. Suddenly, out of nowhere, he is assaulted. At first neither the reader nor Jacob knows who the assailant is; the narrative will not allow us to know too much. A "man" wrestles with him (v. 24). It is not until the aftermath that this shadowy figure is recognized as God (v. 31).

The encounter in the night is a dangerous one. In Chinese the character for "danger" is the same as that for "opportunity." In scripture danger and opportunity are flip sides of the same coin. This is a crisis situation and Jacob must fight for his life, but when it is over, he has more life than he could imagine. Jacob cannot talk his way out, worry his way out, appease this figure in any way. He does not get what he asks for ("Please tell me your name"). He gets instead a lifelong limp and a new name.

A Name and a Blessing

It is not uncommon for people to be given new names in the Bible. The Hebrew name is the identity, submerged for a while, then brought to the surface by God and made clear. Abram, "exalted ancestor," is really Abraham, "ancestor of a multitude" (Gen. 17:5). The name says something deep and telling about the character of that person. Naming is powerful. Furthermore, to know a person's name is to have a secret and hidden knowledge, a degree of control over that person, as well. In Jewish life today, when a person is very sick, his or her Hebrew name may be changed to make it harder for death to find that person. "What's in a name? that which we call a rose / By any other name would smell as sweet," wrote Shakespeare. Hebrew wisdom would counter: This may be true for roses, but not for much else.

📖 Want to Know More?

About the episode of Jacob wrestling with God? See Walter Brueggemann, *Genesis,* Interpretation, 266–74; for a provocative interpretation, see Jack Miles, "Jacob's Wrestling Match: Was It an Angel or Esau?" *Bible Review,* October 1998, 22–23.

About the giving of names? See Paul J. Achtemeier, *Harper's Bible Dictionary* (San Francisco: Harper & Row, 1986), 682–84.

For this reason the stranger does not reveal his name. Jacob wants to have a hold on this character that only knowledge of the name will give him. But the stranger will not give it and cannot be overcome. While Jacob wants power and control, he is given a new name instead.

The name is "Israel." The old Jacob (heel, trickster) does not vanish with the dawn, but he is renamed. His character remains intact:

he grasps the heel of Esau as they enter the world (25:26), he grapples and holds on tight to the dark figure in the night. He is still and always Jacob. He will never be anything else. But something new has happened that will be his forever. Jacob/Israel has been severely touched by God.

"You shall no longer be called Jacob, but Israel, for you have striven with God and with humans, and have prevailed" (32:28). Faith means wrestling with God. The opposite of love is not hate, but apathy. We argue with those whom we love because we love them. We strive to stay engaged and connected when the easy way is letting go. The opposite of faith is not wrestling and struggle, but meek submission. We do well to note that in the story of Job, it is not the pious words of his friends that God loves but the questions and challenges that Job offered up (Job 42:7). Had either Job or Jacob said "You win," they might as well have said "Whatever" or "Que sera, sera." This is fatalism, not faith. As the dark angel tells him, Israel denotes one who has struggled with God and held his own. From here on out, the names Jacob and Israel are used interchangeably for both this man and a nation, which descends from Jacob's twelve sons.

Jacob holds his own. He will not let go. He asks for a blessing, somehow knowing that this otherworldly figure is capable of giving it. The request is ignored at first. Then, as the dawn begins to break, it is granted: "And there he blessed him" (32:29). What is the content of the blessing? Is it the new name? Is it simply the end of the match? How are we to understand it? A clue comes from what Jacob calls this place: Peniel. Peniel (also called Penuel) means "the face of God." The blessing is that Jacob sees God face to face, yet his life is preserved (v. 30).

> **"Bless me"**
>
> "Many of us, like Jacob, have wrestled with something, for something, without really knowing what we sought. Jacob, having now finally gotten ahold of God, finds what he was seeking, and refuses to let go."— John C. L. Gibson, *Genesis*, vol. 2, Daily Study Bible (Philadelphia: Westminster Press, 1982), 200–202.

The long night is almost over, but the sun has not yet risen. Darkness still shrouds the stranger. God's hidden "face" does not protect the divinity, but rather protects us in our frailty. The stranger/God cannot let Jacob see him, as in Exodus 33:20: "You cannot see my face; for no one shall see me and live." The concern here is not for the Holy One but for humans, who must be shielded from the holiness that annihilates in its pure flame. The distance is necessary. Dawn was about to break; he must make haste and be gone! But in the twilight, exhausted Jacob knows who this "man" is. Who let go first? We cannot tell. Perhaps the stranger left freely, or perhaps Jacob permitted him to go. Either way the stranger leaves before the full light of day, and this is a good thing. So the blessing is twofold: Jacob is blessed with a glimpse of the face of God, and he lives to tell the tale.

An Unexpected Welcome

He is limping now toward Esau (33:1), the angry brother with four hundred soldiers, or so he thinks. But Jacob never planned for this: it is a huge reunion, and Esau has let out all the stops. Esau forgets all decorum, hikes up his cloak, and runs to meet his long-lost twin (33:4, compare Luke 15:20). The "army" is there to hold up the welcome-home banner. Esau hugs and kisses him, weeping tears of joy, while Jacob weeps tears of sheer relief.

> "The limping of Penu'el may keep us from speaking flippantly about the 'New Being,' for the New Creature may be marked by limping as the sign of newness (compare 2 Cor. 4:7–12)."—Walter Brueggemann, *Genesis*, Interpretation, 273.

Jacob is overwhelmed. It is not unlike his first meeting with lovely Rachel at the well, when straightaway he fell for her, impulsively kissed her, and let his heart have its way (29:11). To Esau he speaks from the heart as he exclaims, "Truly to see your face is like seeing the face of God" (33:10). It is a shining moment. His is a dazzling, life-giving recognition.

The Holy One is not to be confused with the brother. Between the two there is distance and mystery. And yet the blessing at Peniel is mirrored in the forgiving brother. Jacob spontaneously senses the reflection, some correspondence between heaven and earth. The sacred and the secular, the face of God and the face of Esau, play off one another in a shimmering display.

The reunion was not what Jacob expected. He got the award for "Traveled Farthest to Get Here," but his rehearsed speech stayed crumpled up in the blazer pocket. There never was an opportunity to flash the roll of bills with all the hugging going on. He forgot to be conscious of his thinning hair, and even his bad limp went unnoticed. The funny thing was that name tag he wore:

> "He had met God in the river and in his brother's arms. And God's name and face was Grace."—H. Stephen Shoemaker, *GodStories: New Narratives from Sacred Texts* (Valley Forge, Pa.: Judson Press, 1998), 57.

whoever printed it spelled it right, but somehow the old name didn't seem to fit anymore. And at times, the faces in the crowd seemed to glow. It must have been the candles.

? Questions for Reflection

1. This is a story with many interesting twists and turns (no pun intended). Perhaps most interesting is Esau's welcome of Jacob after Jacob had stolen Esau's birthright and blessing. Why do you think Esau responded to Jacob this way?
2. Jacob has always been a wrestler, struggling with Esau in their mother's womb and then manipulating circumstances and people all along life's way. What is the message of grace to someone who approaches life as a wrestler like Jacob?
3. Jacob is given a new name, and throughout scripture, the faithful are given new names (see even Rev. 2:17). What does it mean to be given a new name? Think of the people who are important in your life. What name would you give them?
4. This is a dramatic moment in Jacob's life—he is reconciled with his brother after many years of separation and has a new relationship with God. What would you think the rest of his life is like? Look over the next few chapters of Genesis to see how accurate you were. Drawing on the previous unit, consider how the next few chapters of Genesis affirm the notion of "being kept by God."

10 Genesis 45:1–28 and 50:15–21

Joseph Makes Himself Known; The Reconciliation of Jacob's Sons

It all starts with a dream.

The dream is of God, as Genesis dreams are. It was given to a boy, then spoken by this boy to his older brothers. It is a curious dream that sets in motion the entire narrative of Genesis 37–50.

As the narrative begins, Joseph is not particularly likable, and the content of the dream increases our hunch that being around him was an unpleasant experience. His father already dotes on him too much for his own good. If this dream is to be believed, he will become the one to whom all will fall down. He will have power. This power is of God. Truly, God's ways are not our ways if this spoiled, insensitive boy is the recipient of such a vision.

"A sheaf of wheat"

We can see him running to his brothers after his long night's sleep. They are up early, doing chores, being good, working the fields. His brilliantly colored coat is flapping and he is beaming with the news. Energetically, he calls them to come listen: their sheaves in the field bowed down to his sheaf (37:7), then later the sun, moon, and eleven stars bowed down to him (37:9). The dream is a doublet, which means it is doubly sure to happen. It is doubly odious to the brothers.

The Plot to Get Rid of Joseph

It is not at all surprising that the brothers find no comfort in his report. All are sons of Jacob, but by four different mothers, and they know their father's favorite wife was Rachel. Joseph is the child of Jacob's old age, and his mother, Rachel, is dead. The triangle between Joseph, his brothers, and Jacob is already loaded with tension. The dream electrifies this tension and ignites the brothers' plan.

Their plotting involves some discussion. The brothers' first plan is to kill him, next to throw him in a pit. Finally they take advantage of a caravan traveling their way and sell Joseph to the traders. As the caravan makes its way to Egypt, the brothers callously show the blood-stained coat to their father. Henceforth Jacob is broken-hearted and inconsolable (37:34, 35). His grief is shocking and immense, so great that no doubt the brothers would retrace their steps if they could. But the evil deed has been done.

The Godly Dreamer

Meanwhile Joseph is sold into slavery, where by fits and starts he rises to power as second-in-command to Pharaoh, the king of Egypt. Taken from home as a teenager, Joseph is thirty when he is put in charge of a huge famine relief program. In the interim he has been falsely accused of attempted rape, imprisoned on that charge, and confined for some time.

It is a gift from God, the ability to interpret dreams, that accounts for his rise to power. In prison Joseph's gift is made known first to his fellow prisoners, then eventually to Pharaoh. Not only does he predict a great famine in the land, he shrewdly devises steps to protect the population and nullify its effects. The narrator makes it clear that "the LORD was with him, and whatever he did, the LORD made it prosper" (39:23). Through adversity the spoiled teenager grows into a wise, successful, and highly moral man. When framed by Potiphar's wife, he asks, "How could I do this great wickedness, and sin against God?" (39:9)

The Reunion

The horror of the brothers' vengeance lingers at home, with their father in perpetual misery. To this horror is added the distress of famine in Canaan. Meanwhile Egypt enjoys storehouses of grain built up under Joseph's command. It has been twenty-two years since the dream. Sent by Jacob to buy grain, the brothers find themselves face to face with this foreigner, who looks and speaks Egyptian, and they bow down (42:6). The dream is enacted as they unwittingly prostrate themselves before Joseph.

Joseph recognizes them of course. He treats them like strangers and speaks harshly, through an interpreter, accusing them of espionage and then throwing them in prison for a few days. After releasing the brothers, Joseph keeps Simeon in Egypt as hostage. He sends the rest home to Canaan with instructions to return with young Benjamin, Joseph's only full brother. Again they make the journey to Egypt, again they are tried, and this time Benjamin is held hostage. The situation parallels the one with Joseph years ago. Will Benjamin likewise be lost to Jacob forever? Can the brothers possibly leave Benjamin behind? Can they tell their father that he has now lost both of Rachel's sons?

It is at this point (44:18) that Judah steps up and delivers one of the finest speeches in all of scripture. He quickly tells this foreign lord a history both know all too well. Judah's focus is on the father, for it is a sure thing that Jacob cannot survive yet another loss. The brother's plan many years ago pushed Jacob to the edge; if Benjamin doesn't return to Canaan, their father will fall into the abyss. Judah offers himself as a slave in Benjamin's place (44:33). The father's well-being is paramount.

> "He who had first suggested selling Joseph into slavery was now willing to become a slave himself in order that Benjamin might be set free to return to his father."—Page H. Kelley, *Journey to the Land of Promise: Genesis–Deuteronomy* (Macon, Ga.: Smyth & Helwys, 1997), 58.

Everything in this carefully crafted narrative leads up to chapter 45. The tale reads so well that we forget we are still in the book of Genesis; up to this point of disclosure we are hardly aware that this story is indeed God's story. The plot flows from dreams in Canaan to dream interpretation in Egypt, from brother banished to littlest brother entrapped, from calculating and deadly plots to impulsive and life-giving speech. The narrator reminds us from time to time that the Lord's hand is in all this, but the players are unaware. At times the brothers ponder: "What is this that God has done to us?" (42:28) after being framed, and "God has found out [our] guilt" (44:16) after Benjamin is held hostage. But the hand of God is not apparent to them, or Joseph, until now.

Joseph is deeply moved by Judah's speech; inside him something shifts. He clears out the Egyptian bodyguards, weeps so loudly they hear him anyway, and declares, "I am Joseph" (45:3). The news is stunning. The brother they thought was dead is very much alive. Just as the disciples were terrified at the end of Mark's Gospel (16:8), so are the brothers shocked by the disclosure. They would expect the worst from this news. Here they are, far from home, face to face with the one whom they betrayed. The guilt they thought would

> "The family is suddenly set in a new context. Their presumed world has been irreversibly shattered."—Walter Brueggemann, *Genesis*, Interpretation, 344.

never go away, that they had lived with for all these years, is finally exposed. Only the death of their father could be more awful than this.

By the Hand of God

Joseph's speech in 45:4–13 is majestic, regal. It is the speech of one who has power and the wisdom to use it well. He comforts the brothers (v. 5), then gives them the real news, news that makes his self-disclosure minor in comparison. He pulls the curtain to reveal not only his identity, but the hand of God:

"God sent me before you to preserve life" (v. 5)
"God sent me before you to preserve for you a remnant on earth" (v. 7)
"It was not you who sent me here, but God" (v. 8)
"God has made me lord of all Egypt" (v. 9)

This announcement is an inspired speech. While the narrator and the reader both know that God's plan has always been at work, neither Joseph nor his brothers know this until now. The words well up from deep inside. He is no longer detached. Joseph can no longer look dispassionately on his brothers, trick them, play them like chess pieces. Nor can he continue to shove his father's grief to the back of his mind (why has he not contacted Jacob after all these years?). His speech is masterful, clear, and full of passion. It has all been worth it, it has all come to this moment, and the awareness breaks in on all the brothers (including Joseph) with astonishing lucidity.

God is purposeful, involved, active, engaged. The brothers plotted; God

> "Almost as much as it is the story of how Israel was saved from famine and extinction, it is the story of how Joseph was saved as a human being."—Frederick Buechner, *Peculiar Treasures: A Biblical Who's Who* (San Francisco: Harper & Row, 1979), 79.

planned. Joseph trapped and tricked his brothers; God touched hearts and stirred history. God works in spite of human effort and through events that appear to have their own rules and logic. The story, up until now, is a Horatio Alger "pull yourself up by your bootstraps" account. It could be a success chronicle out of an Egyptian or American history book. But what is suddenly made clear to both Joseph and the rest of us is that mundane matters are not what they seem. Behind the appearance is the reality of the will of God.

> "The purposes of God have been at work 'in, with, and under' these sordid human actions."—Walter Brueggemann, *Genesis, Interpretation*, 346.

Even Things Not Seen

God's sovereignty is the issue here. If the rule of God is understood as compulsion, we miss the point: God's omnipotence is then coercive and tyrannical, while humans are automatons programmed to do "God's will" as if this were set in stone (or hard-wired into us). But other models for sovereignty and power are made available to us through the biblical text, and Joseph's speech makes this clear. God's rule allows for free human agency. The will of God does not force itself on creation. Instead, as in Genesis 1, God calls and coaxes creation into being.

"You sold me here" is true; "God sent me before you" is also true. God's sovereignty is known through God's lovingkindness, which draws the family together ("Come closer to me") and makes the disclosure possible. It does not compel; it invites. The freedom of humans to respond to God's sovereignty or not is maintained. But their actions have been drawn into God's larger purpose for the good. The loving will of God makes use of all human action.

The earlier chapters of Genesis tell us of the God who appears and speaks, who intervenes and intrudes. God is up front and center in the great sweep of primeval history, certainly, and in the narrower arena of patriarchal history. God visits Abraham repeatedly and haggles with him over the fate of Sodom. God appears to Jacob in a dream, then later comes as the dark angel to wrestle with him in the night. But the Joseph story has none of these elements.

In Joseph's world, which feels so much like our own, dramatic religious elements are absent. There is no call of God, no discussion with God, no appearance of God. Nothing is direct or explicit here

at all. Our culture resonates with the world of Joseph-in-Egypt, a profane and secular world where it seems "obvious" that God no longer
addresses us with direct speech and ex-
traordinary promises. There is no plea
for faith or response to God in the
Joseph narrative. But there is, finally and
fully in chapter 45, the amazed affirmation that this narrative has been God's
story, in and through and despite human activity.

> "As for you, you meant evil against me, but God meant it for good." (RSV)

It was God acting in this family, beginning with the dream, then
moving through and past the brothers' gruesome plot. God propelled
the rise to power, giving Joseph the uncanny knack of interpreting
dreams. It was God stirring the heart of Judah to his famous speech.
Looking back through the lens of faith, the past is made clear. Joseph
is able to see his story for what it truly is: "So it was not you who sent
me here, but God."

Thy Will Be Done

For Pharaoh and the Egyptian empire, such an affirmation cannot be
made. This shrewd foreigner has saved them all from famine. They
do not know that they have been blessed through Abraham's family
by God (Gen. 12:3: "in you all the families of the earth shall be
blessed"). For Pharaoh and his household, what has just happened is
simply a happy coincidence. They are pleased (v. 16), and they act
with hospitality and magnanimity toward this foreign family. There
is no recognition on their part of the sovereignty of God or providence at work. Pharaoh's graciousness is his own. And yet, it is God's
as well.

It is God who will act in the future by preserving life and by keeping a remnant on earth. This theme is echoed in Isaiah when centuries
later, God promises that after destruction of Israel a remnant will return from exile (Isa. 10:21). The agent of the return will be, like
Pharaoh, a foreigner. Cyrus of Persia will be the Lord's anointed, and
his right hand will be guided by God. Incredibly, the Lord says of
Cyrus: "I call you by your name, I surname you, though you do not
know me" (Isa. 45:4). Whether or not Pharaoh, Cyrus, or we today
know it is so, God's purposes will grow to fruition. "God's will be
done," we pray, and we do well to acknowledge that such is in fact
going on as we speak.

The psalmist acknowledges that God's will is done:

> The LORD brings the counsel of the nations to nothing;
>   he frustrates the plans of the peoples.
> The counsel of the LORD stands forever,
>   the thoughts of his heart to all generations.
>   (Ps. 33:10–11)

The wisdom literature of Proverbs likewise acknowledges this truth:

> The human mind may devise many plans,
>   but it is the purpose of the LORD that will be established.
>   (Prov. 19:21)

The Joseph story is an enactment of this conviction.

 Want to Know More?

About Joseph's coat? See Gerhard von Rad, *Genesis*, revised ed., Old Testament Library (Philadelphia: Westminster Press, 1973), 351.

About the use of garments in the Joseph stories? See Page H. Kelley, *Journey to the Land of Promise: Genesis–Deuteronomy* (Macon, Ga.: Smyth & Helwys, 1997), 53–54.

About famine? See Paul J. Achtemeier, *Harper's Bible Dictionary* (San Francisco: Harper & Row, 1985), 303.

About the sovereignty of God? See Shirley C. Guthrie, *Christian Doctrine*, revised ed. (Louisville, Ky.: Westminster John Knox Press, 1994), 166–91.

For the immediate future, Jacob and his large family will settle in Goshen, a fertile land in Egypt's Delta, and prosper. The grief of the father will end. Joseph fills the role of provider and comforter, but now they all know that the real provider is God.

The Brothers Plot Again

The scene shifts to chapter 50. Seventeen years have passed. The family has settled in Egypt, where they are richly blessed. As God intended in Genesis 1:28, they are fruitful and they "multiply exceedingly" (47:27). Joseph's sons, Ephraim and Manasseh, are adopted by Jacob. Finally, after a long and eventful life, Jacob blesses his children on his deathbed. A huge entourage takes his body back to Abraham's cave at Machpelah, where Jacob is laid to rest.

With Jacob's death comes a major shift in the family dynamic. The guilt of the brothers, buried for years, wells back up. What if? What if their powerful brother has buried his resentment for all these years? What if their betrayal of Joseph still defines the family relationship? What if the commanding father, now dead, was their only security?

As it always is with guilt, the past looms larger than life. They suppose that the past, *their* past, is the only reality. Revenge is Joseph's to wreak, and he holds all the cards.

Once again they make a plan. They gather in anxiety to discuss the new situation, now one without the patriarch to protect them. They approach Joseph (50:16; the NIV has it more indirectly: "they sent word to him"). They report their father's wishes, which were unknown until this moment, that Joseph forgive them the crime of long ago. Whether this message is a fabrication or not, the timing is significant. Joseph does not know the message, and he weeps when he hears it. And the dream of chapter 37, enacted in 42:6, 43:26, 44:14, recurs once again and for the last time. His brothers throw themselves down before him and cry, "We are . . . your slaves" (50:18).

The Transforming Power of God

The relationship between them is exactly what was foretold by Joseph in chapter 37. And this time, the dream is not what Joseph wants at all. The shock of seeing his prostrated brothers (who should bow to no one but God!) impels him to claim once again the recognition of chapter 45: "God intended it for good." In spite of the brothers' evil intent, good has been done. Faith understands this. The designs of humans can really be for evil, their actions can really be free, and yet the intent of God will prevail. In the twentieth century, when war and genocide seem to have had the last word, the biblical witness takes our breath away. It seems too good to be true; it is too good not to be true.

> "This 'believing' is no simplistic notion that the evil we see in the world is not truly evil, but some form of hidden good. Rather, it is the stubborn faith that there is no evil dark enough that God somehow, someway, sometime cannot redeem."—H. Stephen Shoemaker, *GodStories: New Narratives from Sacred Texts* (Valley Forge, Pa.: Judson Press, 1998), 67.

Give God the glory! Fall down, not in front of a human being, but before God! Joseph cannot utter the words of forgiveness because they are not his to give. Forgiveness is the Lord's, as Joseph reminds them: "Am I in the place of God?" From Joseph's perspective the wrong they have done him years ago has vanished, leaving him in a position of power. Or better, the wrong has been transformed, giving Joseph the ability to save the lives of many. Faith looks at God's work in the past and says, "As incredible as it sounds, I wouldn't have had it any other way."

Instead Joseph gives them what they really need from him, and these are words of comfort. "Do not be afraid! . . . Have no fear." He speaks to them kindly, moving the family into the future. Joseph the powerful one will continue to provide for them and theirs, even to the third generation of great-grandchildren. The family stands together under the protection of God, and reconciliation has occurred.

When it is his time to die (50:24), Joseph asks one and only one thing. The brothers must swear to bury him back in the land promised to their great-grandfather Abraham. Genesis ends with their oath (50:25). They will carry his bones back home. Joshua 24:32 confirms that four centuries later, the oath was remembered and his request was honored.

And God Saw That It Was Good

It all started with a dream, planned first in the mind of God. It ends with the dream fulfilled and a whole new orientation: the brothers' long-buried guilt is uprooted and aired, the spoiled son becomes one who uses his power for the greater good. Intentional evil is transformed into the deliberate blessing of Egypt, the family, and the future nation of Israel. The plan of God is on the side of life and always for good.

With the end of Genesis we are brought back to the beginning: "God saw everything that he had made, and indeed, it was very good" (1:31). We come full circle and look at creation anew. The intent of all creation is not perfection but goodness, not a static unchanging ideal but growth into maturity. What has begun will grow to fruition. This is what God has been doing all along, both overtly (with Abraham and Jacob) and discreetly, covertly, powerfully (in the Joseph story). At our best, we participate with God in that pursuit of goodness. Yet, thanks be to God, God's purposes do not cease even in the face of human failure and frailty. The Genesis story is that of God's consistent, overriding purpose from beginning to end: that there be life, and it be good.

> "The narrative now comes to a conclusion. But Genesis is not an ending. It is a beginning."—Walter Brueggemann, *Genesis*, Interpretation, 369.

? Questions for Reflection

1. Joseph has a tremendous gift—the ability to foretell the future and the ability to interpret dreams. Unfortunately, his impetuous revelation of his gift to his brothers nearly gets him killed. What are some gifts you recognize in others? What are some ways that gifts can be misused?
2. The interplay between brothers in Genesis is interesting. Think back over the units of this study. How many of them involve the relationship of brothers? What are the different situations and common themes among the stories?
3. Joseph forgives his brothers twice (as if the brothers don't believe it the first time). How often does the message of forgiveness need to be given so that it is heard and believed? Why?
4. "Even though you intended to do harm to me, God intended it for good" is a compelling conclusion to the Joseph story, and the story of Genesis. What began on the first day of creation, continues on now into the exodus. Looking back on all the events of Genesis, what does it mean to "be good"?

Bibliography

Brueggemann, Walter. *Genesis.* Interpretation. Atlanta: John Knox Press, 1982.

Heschel, Abraham Joshua. *The Sabbath.* New York: Farrar, Straus & Giroux, 1951.

Niditch, Susan. "Genesis." In *Women's Bible Commentary,* expanded edition, edited by Carol A. Newsom and Sharon H. Ringe. Louisville, Ky.: Westminster John Knox Press, 1998.

Palmer, Parker. *The Company of Strangers.* New York: Crossroad 1981.

Telushkin, Joseph. *Jewish Literacy.* New York: William Morrow & Co., 1991.

Interpretation Bible Studies
Leader's Guide

Interpretation Bible Studies (IBS), for adults and older youth, are flexible, attractive, easy-to-use, and filled with solid information about the Bible. IBS helps Christians discover the guidance and power of the scriptures for living today. Perhaps you are leading a church school class, a mid-week Bible study group, or a youth group meeting, or simply using this in your own personal study. Whatever the setting may be, we hope you find this *Leader's Guide* helpful. Since every context and group is different, this *Leader's Guide* does not presume to tell you how to structure Bible study for your situation. Instead, the *Leader's Guide* seeks to offer choices— a number of helpful suggestions for leading a successful Bible study using IBS.

> "The traditioning process, when it is faithful, must be disciplined, critical, and informed by the best intelligence of the day. But it must be continued—and is continued—each time we meet in synagogue or church for telling and sharing, for reading and study, each time we present ourselves for new disclosure 'fresh from the Word.'"—Walter Brueggemann, *Introduction to the Old Testament*, 2nd ed. (Louisville, Ky.: Westminster John Knox Press, 2012), 10.

How Should I Teach IBS?

1. Explore the Format

There is a wealth of information in IBS, perhaps more than you can use in one session. In this case, more is better. IBS has been designed to give you a well-stocked buffet of content and teachable insights. Pick and choose what suits your group's needs. Perhaps you will want to split units into two or more sessions, or combine units into a single session.

Perhaps you will decide to use only a portion of a unit and then move on to the next unit. *There is not a structured theme or teaching focus to each unit that must be followed for IBS to be used.* Rather, IBS offers the flexibility to adjust to whatever suits your context.

"The more we bring to the Bible, the more we get from the Bible."—William Barclay, *A Beginner's Guide to the New Testament* (Louisville, Ky.: Westminster John Knox Press, 1995), vii.

A recent survey of both professional and volunteer church educators revealed that their number-one concern was that Bible study materials be teacher-friendly. IBS is indeed teacher-friendly in two important ways. First, since IBS provides abundant content and a flexible design, teachers can shape the lessons creatively, responding to the needs of the group and employing a wide variety of teaching methods. Second, those who wish more specific suggestions for planning the sessions can find them at the Westminster John Knox Press Web site (**www.wjkbooks.com**). Here, you can access a study guide with teaching suggestions for each IBS unit as well as helpful quotations, selections from Bible dictionaries and encyclopedias, and other teaching helps.

IBS is not only teacher-friendly but also discussion-friendly. Given the opportunity, most adults and young people relish the chance to talk about the kind of issues raised in IBS. The secret, then, is to determine what works with your group, what will get them to talk. Several good methods for stimulating discussion are presented in this *Leader's Guide,* and once you learn your group, you can apply one of these methods and get the group discussing the Bible and its relevance in their lives.

The format of every IBS unit consists of several features:

a. **Body of the Unit.** This is the main content, consisting of interesting and informative commentary on the passage and scholarly insight into the biblical text and its significance for Christians today.

b. **Sidebars.** These are boxes that appear scattered throughout the body of the unit, with maps, photos, quotations, and intriguing ideas. Some sidebars can be identified quickly by a symbol, or icon, that helps the reader know what type of information can be found in that sidebar. There are icons for illustrations, key terms, pertinent quotes, and more.

c. **Want to Know More?** Each unit includes a "Want to Know More?" section that guides learners who wish to dig deeper and consult other resources. If your church library does not have the resources mentioned, you can look up the information in other standard Bible dictionaries, encyclopedias, and handbooks, or you can find much of this information at the Westminster John Knox Press Web site (see last page of this Guide).

d. Questions for Reflection. The unit ends with questions to help the learners think more deeply about the biblical passage and its pertinence for today. These questions are provided as examples only, and teachers are encouraged both to develop their own list of questions and to gather questions from the group. These discussion questions do not usually have specific "correct" answers. Again, the flexibility of IBS allows you to use these questions at the end of the group time, at the beginning, interspersed throughout, or not at all.

> "On the very first occasion when someone stood up in public to tell people about Jesus, he made it very clear: this message is for everyone. That message is as true today as it was then." —N. T. Wright, *Matthew for Everyone, Part 2* (Louisville, Ky.: Westminster John Knox Press, 2004), ix.

2. Select a Teaching Method

Here are ten suggestions. The format of IBS allows you to choose what direction you will take as you plan to teach. Only you will know how your lesson should best be designed for your group. Some adult groups prefer the lecture method, while others prefer a high level of free-ranging discussion. Many youth groups like interaction, activity, the use of music, and the chance to talk about their own experiences and feelings. Here is a list of a few possible approaches. Let your own creativity add to the list!

a. Let's Talk about What We've Learned. In this approach, all group members are requested to read the scripture passage and the IBS unit before the group meets. Ask the group members to make notes about the main issues, concerns, and questions they see in the passage. When the group meets, these notes are collected, shared, and discussed. This method depends, of course, on the group's willingness to do some "homework."

b. What Do We Want and Need to Know? This approach begins by having the whole group read the scripture passage together. Then, drawing from your study of the IBS, you, as the teacher, write on a board or flip chart two lists:

(1) Things we should know to better understand this passage (content information related to the passage, for example, historical insights about political contexts, geographical landmarks, economic nuances, etc.), and

(2) Four or five "important issues we should talk about regarding this passage" (with implications for today— how the issues in the biblical context continue into today, for example, issues of idolatry or fear).

> "Although small groups can meet for many purposes and draw upon many different resources, the one resource which has shaped the life of the Church more than any other throughout its long history has been the Bible."—Roberta Hestenes, *Using the Bible in Groups* (Philadelphia: Westminster Press, 1983), 14.

Allow the group to add to either list, if they wish, and use the lists to lead into a time of learning, reflection, and discussion. This approach is suitable for those settings where there is little or no advanced preparation by the students.

c. Hunting and Gathering. Start the unit by having the group read the scripture passage together. Then divide the group into smaller clusters (perhaps having as few as one person), each with a different assignment. Some clusters can discuss one or more of the "Questions for Reflection." Others can look up key terms or people in a Bible dictionary or track down other biblical references found in the body of the unit. After the small clusters have had time to complete their tasks, gather the entire group again and lead them through the study material, allowing each cluster to contribute what it learned.

d. From Question Mark to Exclamation Point. This approach begins with contemporary questions and then moves to the biblical content as a response to those questions. One way to do this is for you to ask the group, at the beginning of the class, a rephrased version of one or more of the "Questions for Reflection" at the end of the study unit. For example, one of the questions at the end of the unit on Exodus 3:1–4:17 in the IBS *Exodus* volume reads,

> Moses raised four protests, or objections, to God's call. Contemporary people also raise objections to God's call. In what ways are these similar to Moses' protests? In what ways are they different?

This question assumes familiarity with the biblical passage about Moses, so the question would not work well before the group has explored the passage. However, try rephrasing this question as an opening exercise; for example:

Here is a thought experiment: Let's assume that God, who called people in the Bible to do daring and risky things, still calls people today to tasks of faith and courage. In the Bible, God called Moses from a burning bush and called Isaiah in a moment of ecstatic worship in the Temple. How do you think God's call is experienced by people today? Where do you see evidence of people saying "yes" to God's call? When people say "no" or raise an objection to God's call, what reasons do they give (to themselves, to God)?

Posing this or a similar question at the beginning will generate discussion and raise important issues, and then it can lead the group into an exploration of the biblical passage as a resource for thinking even more deeply about these questions.

e. Let's Go to the Library. From your church library, your pastor's library, or other sources, gather several good commentaries on the book of the Bible you are studying. Among the trustworthy commentaries are those in the Interpretation series (Westminster John Knox Press) and the Westminster Bible Companion series (Westminster John Knox Press). Divide your groups into smaller clusters and give one commentary to each cluster (one or more of the clusters can be given the IBS volume instead of a full-length commentary). Ask each cluster to read the biblical passage you are studying and then to read the section of the commentary that covers that passage (if your group is large, you may want to make photocopies of the commentary material with proper permission, of course). The task of each cluster is to name the two or three most important insights they discover about the biblical passage by reading and talking together about the commentary material. When you reassemble the larger group to share these insights, your group will gain not only a variety of insights about the passage but also a sense that differing views of the same text are par for the course in biblical interpretation.

f. Working Creatively Together. Begin with a creative group task, tied to the main thrust of the study. For example, if the study is on the Ten Commandments, a parable, or a psalm, have the group rewrite the Ten Commandments, the parable, or the psalm in contemporary language. If the passage is an epistle, have the group write a letter to their own congregation. Or if the study is a narrative, have the group role-play the characters in the story or write a page describing the story from the point of view of one of the characters. After completion of the task, read and discuss the biblical passage, asking for interpretations and applications from the group and tying in IBS material as it fits the flow of the discussion.

g. Singing Our Faith. Begin the session by singing (or reading) together a hymn that alludes to the biblical passage being studied (or to the theological themes in the passage). For example, if you are studying the unit from the IBS volume on Psalm 121, you can sing "I to the Hills Will Lift My Eyes," "Sing Praise to God, Who Reigns Above," or another hymn based on Psalm 121. Let the group reflect on the thoughts and feelings evoked by the hymn, then move to the biblical passage, allowing the biblical text and the IBS material to underscore, clarify, refine, and deepen the discussion stimulated by the hymn. If you are ambitious, you may ask the group to write a new hymn at the end of the study! (Many hymnals have indexes in the back or companion volumes that help the user match hymns to scripture passages or topics.)

h. Fill in the Blanks. In order to help the learners focus on the content of the biblical passage, at the beginning of the session ask each member of the group to read the biblical passage and fill out a brief questionnaire about the details of the passage (provide a copy for each learner or write the questions on the board). For example, if you are studying the unit in the IBS *Matthew* volume on Matthew 22:1–14, the questionnaire could include questions such as the following:

—In this story, Jesus compares the kingdom of heaven to what?
—List the various responses of those who were invited to the king's banquet but who did not come.
—When his invitation was rejected, how did the king feel? What did the king do?
—In the second part of the story, when the king saw a man at the banquet without a wedding garment, what did the king say? What did the man say? What did the king do?
—What is the saying found at the end of this story?

Gather the group's responses to the questions and perhaps encourage discussion. Then lead the group through the IBS material, helping the learners to understand the meanings of these details and the significance of the passage for today. Feeling creative? Instead of a fill-in-the-blanks questionnaire, create a crossword puzzle from names and words in the biblical passage.

i. Get the Picture. In this approach, stimulate group discussion by incorporating a painting, photograph, or other visual object into the lesson. You can begin by having the group examine and comment on this visual, or you can introduce the visual later in the lesson—it depends on the object used. If, for example, you are studying the unit Exodus 3:1–4:17 in the IBS *Exodus* volume, you may want to view Paul Koli's very colorful painting *The Burning Bush.* Two sources for this painting are *The Bible through Asian Eyes,* edited by Masao Takenaka and Ron O'Grady (National City, Calif.: Pace Publishing Co., 1991), and *Imaging the Word: An Arts and Lectionary Resource,* vol. 3, edited by Susan A. Blain (Cleveland: United Church Press, 1996).

j. Now Hear This. Especially if your class is large, you may want to use the lecture method. As the teacher, you prepare a presentation on the biblical passage, using as many resources as you have available plus your own experience, but following the content of the IBS unit as a guide. You can make the lecture even more lively by asking the learners at various points along the way to refer to the visuals and quotes found in the "sidebars." A place can be made for questions (like the ones at the end of the unit)—either at the close of the lecture or at strategic points along the way.

> "It is a mistake to look to the Bible to close a discussion; the Bible seeks to open one."—William Sloane Coffin, *Credo* (Louisville, Ky.: Westminster John Knox Press, 2004), 145.

3. Keep These Teaching Tips in Mind

There are no surefire guarantees for a teaching success. However, the following suggestions can increase the chances for a successful study:

a. Always Know Where the Group Is Headed. Take ample time beforehand to prepare the material. Know the main points of the study, and know the destination. Be flexible, and encourage discussion, but don't lose sight of where you are headed.

b. Ask Good Questions; Don't Be Afraid of Silence. Ideally, a discussion blossoms spontaneously from the reading of the scripture. But more often than not, a discussion must be drawn from the group members by a series of well-chosen questions. After asking each question, give the group members time to answer. Let them think, and don't be threatened by a season of silence. Don't feel that every question must have an answer and that as leader, you must supply every answer. Facilitate discussion by getting the group members to cooperate with each other. Sometimes the original question can be restated. Sometimes it is helpful to ask a follow-up question like "What makes this a hard question to answer?"

Ask questions that encourage explanatory answers. Try to avoid questions that can be answered simply "Yes" or "No." Rather than asking, "Do you think Moses was frightened by the burning bush?" ask, "What do you think Moses was feeling and experiencing as he stood before the burning bush?" If group members answer with just one word, ask a follow-up question like "Why do you think this is so?" Ask questions about their feelings and opinions, mixed within questions about facts or details. Repeat their responses or restate their response to reinforce their contributions to the group.

> "The whole purpose of the Bible, it seems to me, is to convince people to set the written word down in order to become living words in the world for God's sake. For me, this willing conversion of ink back to blood is the full substance of faith." —Barbara Brown Taylor, *Leaving Church: A Memoir of Faith* (New York: HarperOne, 2007), 107.

Most studies can generate discussion by asking open-ended questions. Depending on the group, several types of questions can work. Some groups will respond well to content questions that can be answered from reading the IBS comments or the biblical passage. Others will respond well to questions about feelings or thoughts. Still others will respond to questions that challenge them to new thoughts or that may not have exact answers. Be sensitive to the group's dynamic in choosing questions.

Some suggested questions are: What is the point of the passage? Who are the main characters? Where is the tension in the story? Why does it say (this) _____, and not (that) _____? What raises questions for you? What terms need defining? What are the new ideas? What doesn't make sense? What bothers or troubles you about this passage? What keeps you from living the truth of this passage?

c. Don't Settle for the Ordinary. There is nothing like a surprise. Think of special or unique ways to present the ideas of the study. Upset the applecart of the ordinary. Even though the passage may be familiar, look for ways to introduce suspense. Remember that a little mystery can capture the imagination. Change your routine.

Along with the element of surprise, humor can open up a discussion. Don't be afraid to laugh. A well-chosen joke or cartoon may present the central theme in a way that a lecture would have stymied.

Sometimes a passage is too familiar. No one speaks up because everyone feels that all that could be said has been said. Choose an unfamiliar translation from which to read, or if the passage is from a Gospel, compare the story across two or more Gospels and note differences. It is amazing what insights can be drawn from seeing something strange in what was thought to be familiar.

d. Feel Free to Supplement the IBS Resources with Other Material. Consult other commentaries or resources. Tie in current events with the lesson. Scour newspapers or magazines for stories that touch on the issues of the study. Sometimes the lyrics of a song, or a section of prose from a well-written novel, will be just the right seasoning for the study. The Thoughtful Christian (www .TheThoughtfulChristian.com) has a multitude of Bible study and teaching material available.

e. And Don't Forget to Check the Web. You can download a free study guide from our Web site (**www.wjkbooks.com**). Each study guide includes several possibilities for applying the teaching methods suggested above for individual IBS units.

f. Stay Close to the Biblical Text. Don't forget that the goal is to learn the Bible. Return to the text again and again. Avoid making the mistake of reading the passage only at the beginning of the study, and then wandering away to comments on top of comments from that point on. Trust in the power

> "The Bible is literature, but it is much more than literature. It is the holy book of Jews and Christians, who find there a manifestation of God's presence."—Kathleen Norris, *The Psalms* (New York: Riverhead Books, 1997), xxii.

and presence of the Holy Spirit to use the truths of the passage to work within the lives of the study participants.

What If I Am Using IBS in Personal Bible Study?

If you are using IBS in your personal Bible study, you can experiment and explore a variety of ways. You may choose to read straight through the study without giving any attention to the sidebars or other features. Or you may find yourself interested in a question or unfamiliar with a key term, and you can allow the sidebars "Want to Know More?" and "Questions for Reflection" to lead you into deeper learning on these issues. Perhaps you will want to have a few commentaries or a Bible dictionary available to pursue what interests you. As was suggested in one of the teaching methods above, you may want to begin with the questions at the end, and then read the Bible passage followed by the IBS material. Trust the IBS resources to provide good and helpful information, and then follow your interests!

📖 Want to Know More?

Studies at The Thoughtful Christian

These studies, which are available at www.TheThoughtfulChristian.com, will help with questions about Bible study, Bible basics, and the development of the Bible:

- "Bible 101," by John A. Cairns
- "Biblical Interpretation 101," by W. Eugene March
- "How to Study a Bible Passage," by Donald L. Griggs
- "The Importance of Context" and "Tools for Bible Study," by Gary W. Light
- "Types of Literature in the Bible" and "When and Why the Bible Was Written," by Emily Cheney
- "Which Bible Should I Buy?" by Steven M. Sheeley

Other Helpful Resources

- *The Bible from Scratch: The Old Testament for Beginners,* by Donald L. Griggs (Louisville, Ky.: Westminster John Knox Press, 2002) and *The Bible from Scratch: The New Testament for Beginners,* by Donald L. Griggs (Louisville, Ky.: Westminster John Knox Press, 2003)
- *How the Bible Came to Be,* by John Barton (Louisville, Ky.: Westminster John Knox Press, 1997)
- *Using the Bible in Groups,* by Roberta Hestenes (Louisville, Ky.: Westminster John Knox Press, 1983)

To download a free IBS study guide,

visit our Web site at

www.wjkbooks.com